W9-AMA-962

FAVORITE MEALS

from Williamsburg

FAVORITE MEALS *from Williamsburg*

A Menu Cookbook

Recipes Compiled and Adapted
by Charlotte Turgeon
and the Staff of
The Colonial Williamsburg Foundation

Donna C. Sheppard, General Editor

Photographs by William K. Sladcik and John Hurt Whitehead

Watercolors and Line Drawings by Vernon Wooten

Colonial Williamsburg
The Colonial Williamsburg Foundation
Williamsburg, Virginia

15 14 13 12 11 10 09 08 10 11 12 13 14 15

Library of Congress Cataloging-in-Publication Data

Turgeon, Charlotte Snyder
Favorite Meals from Williamsburg.

Includes index.
1. Cookery, American—Virginia. 2. Menus.
3. Williamsburg, (Va.)—Social life and customs. I. Sheppard, Donna C. II. Colonial Williamsburg Foundation. III. Title.
TX715.T9147 1982 641.59755 82-4518
ISBN 978-0-87935-066-6 AACR2
ISBN 978-0-87935-067-3 (pbk.)

This book was designed by Vernon Wooten

Printed in China

The Colonial Williamsburg Foundation
PO Box 1776
Williamsburg, VA 23187-1776
www.colonialwilliamsburg.org

Cover:
A succulent Roast Young Tom Turkey garnished with orange baskets holding Cranberry and Orange Relish graces the Tidewater Virginia Thanksgiving table. Green Beans with Surry County Peanuts, Honey and Cinnamon-Candied Yams, Nutmeats and Dried Fruits, and a Virginia Apple Custard Tart complete the feast. A silver epergne piled high with Nature's bounty adds a note of elegance.

Frontispiece:
Zesty Tomato Juice Royale is the perfect beverage to accompany the Cascades Hunt Breakfast, a lavish array of southern favorites that includes (clockwise from upper right) Colonial Buttermilk Biscuits, Hashed Brown Potatoes, Pan Fried Oysters with Spicy Cocktail Sauce, Fried Shenandoah Valley Apple Slices, Scrambled Eggs with Virginia Ham, and Bran Muffins.

Contents

Acknowledgments

Many people have helped create this book. Special thanks go to Chefs Pierre Monet, Rolf Herion, and Ted Kristensen and the staff of the Hotels and Restaurants division at Colonial Williamsburg and to John C. Austin, Susan H. Axtell, Betty Hundley Babb, Sally Barnes, Leslie Brown, Patricia A. Gibbs, Patricia A. Hurdle, Claude Jones, Jr., Anita M. Kordela, Martha Marquardt, Audrey Noël Hume, Harold Page, Susan H. Rountree, Mary Theobald, and George Wilson.

Memorable Meals from Williamsburg, Then and Now

Hospitality, Virginia-style

Memorable meals are as much a part of dining in Williamsburg now as they were two centuries ago when our forefathers gathered here for "Publick Times." *Favorite Meals from Williamsburg* contains 30 suggested menus and 200 recipes that will enable you to re-create many of the most popular dishes served at Colonial Williamsburg's world famous taverns and restaurants.

Hospitality, Virginia-style, has long been associated with the Old Dominion, where Virginians have traditionally kept open house to an extraordinary degree. During colonial days relatives and friends visited back and forth and even strangers were welcome. The mistress of a plantation or house in town prided herself on a well-ordered household in which the dining table occupied a central position. Lavish meals were carefully planned to take advantage of the wide variety of food stuffs available to the eighteenth-century homemaker. Philip Vickers Fithian, tutor to the children of planter Robert Carter at Nomini Hall plantation, recorded some of the dishes at an "elegant dinner" for ten in 1774: "Beef & Greens; roast-Pig; fine boil'd Rock-Fish, Pudding, Cheese &c" washed down with "good Porter-Beer, Cyder, Rum, & Brandy Toddy.

The first settlers at Jamestown found rivers teeming with fish, oysters, crabs, and clams and forests where game was plentiful. Fruits and vegetables flourished in Virginia's favorable climate, as did domestic animals, especially pigs, which provided the distinctively flavored bacon and ham for which the region has long been famous. The Indians contributed corn, which clever housewives turned into hoecakes, ashcakes, and pone. By the time Williamsburg was founded as the capital of the colony in 1699, the colonists truly did enjoy a "groaning board."

Menus in Colonial Days

Because most Virginians were of English and Scottish stock, they ate much the same kinds of food in the New World that Britons favored in the Old. Cookbooks came from England, and Virginia housewives depended on Mrs. Smith, Mrs. Glasse, or Mrs. Raffald for recipes, menus, and advice on how to set their tables. The fifth edition of Mrs. E. Smith's *The Compleat Housewife; or, Accomplish'd Gentlewoman's Companion*, first published in London in 1727, was reprinted for sale by William Parks at the *Virginia Gazette* printing office in Williamsburg in 1742. It is the first cookbook known to have been published in British America and it remained popular throughout the colonial period.

Eighteenth-century cookbooks show a familiarity with such exotic ingredients as anchovies, capers, caviar, truffles, mangos, and a wide spectrum of spices. They also contain a number of recipes that sound strange to a modern ear and probably would not appeal to twentieth-century palates—a "Ragoo of Hogs Feet and Ears," stuffed cockscombs, or gooseberry sauce with mackerel, among others. Pity the poor housewife confronted with the preparation of a Yorkshire Christmas pie, the recipe for which instructed her to stuff a partridge with a pigeon, a

fowl with the partridge, a goose with the fowl, and finally a turkey with the goose, all to be baked in a pastry case made from a bushel of flour and ten pounds of butter. Other recipes required long stirring or beating. Mrs. Raffald's lemon syllabubs had to be whisked for half an hour, and the cook was told to beat the ingredients for a pound cake "well together for one hour with your hand."

Some cooking techniques were different too. Roasts were turned on a spit in front of the huge fireplace; stews simmered in iron pots suspended over the embers; baking often was done on the hearth. Virginia kitchens were usually separate structures in order to keep the heat and smells of cooking away from the house, so the food had to be carried back and forth.

Mealtimes had become fairly standard by the eighteenth century. Breakfast was served at eight or nine o'clock. It consisted of cold sliced meats or a hash, beverages—coffee, tea, chocolate, or milk—and hot breads such as buns, muffins, and corn pone. Many Virginians preferred breads made from cornmeal to those of wheat flour. "Indian cakes for breakfast after the Virginia fashion" were the rule at Mount Vernon, for example.

Dinner was the main meal of the day. Family, friends, and acquaintances gathered at two or three in the afternoon. They enjoyed a sumptuous meal of at least two courses that adhered to well-established conventions. Elaborate diagrams in the cookbooks of the day showed the style conscious hostess how to arrange the dishes on her table in order to show them off to best advantage. A proper table was expected to be balanced from top to bottom, side to side, and at the corners as well. As Mrs. Bradley admonished in her cookbook of circa 1770, "The best Dinner in the World will have an ill Aspect if the Dishes are not properly disposed on the Table."

The first course featured a lavish presentation of meats and garnishes. Instead of today's floral bouquet, the centerpiece was likely to be a huge meat pie in a pastry "coffin" or a calf's head. A Virginia ham was considered ideal for the top of the table, perhaps balanced at the bottom by a joint of beef or venison, a leg of lamb or veal, or by a roast turkey. Soup was served by the mistress, "removed," and replaced with another dish. Other meats—a fricassee of rabbits or marinated pigeons, for example—were held to be suitable "side" dishes, while stewed crab or lobster pie might have appeared at the corners. Vegetables garnished the meat platters or were served separately. Elaborate salads and "made dishes" somewhat akin to modern casseroles also graced the dinner table.

British practice combined additional meat and fish dishes with fruits, sweetmeats, custards, and tarts for the second course, but Virginia housewives seem to have favored a true dessert course. A pyramid of glass salvers piled with containers of jellies, ice creams, syllabubs, and candied fruits centered the table; other desserts were arranged around it. Various beverages, alcoholic or not, were served with both courses.

The day's culinary activities concluded about eight with supper, a light repast of seafood or cold meat and buttered breads, followed by fruit or a sweet dish. Occasionally the tidewater gentry enjoyed an elaborate late-night ball supper. At a ball attended by William Byrd II, master of Westover plantation on the James River, the royal governor danced "a French dance with my wife." Later the guests "danced country dances . . . and the company was carried into another room where was a very fine collation of sweetmeats." In 1746, the Governor's Council and Burgesses gave a victory ball at the Capitol to celebrate the battle of Culloden and served "a very handsome Collation spread on three Tables, in three different rooms, consisting of near 100 Dishes, after the most delicate Taste."

Meals at Williamsburg Today

Taverns have been an important part of the life of Williamsburg for nearly three hundred years, providing food and beverages to hungry and thirsty patrons. Today Christiana Campbell's Tavern, the King's Arms Tavern, Chowning's Tavern, and Shields Tavern are operated much in the manner of those eighteenth-century hostelries.

Chesapeake Bay jambalaya is a specialty at Christiana Campbell's, a tavern frequented by George Washington, who often noted in his diary that he had "dined," "supped," or "spent the evening at Mrs. Campbell's." Mrs. Jane Vobe kept a tavern "at the Sign of the King's Arms" on Duke of Gloucester Street from 1772 to 1785. Considered one of the most genteel in the town, the King's Arms was a favorite of members of the planter aristocracy. Today the King's Arms serves tasty fare that includes Yorkshire meat pies with Yorkshire topping and Mrs. Randolph's frozen lemonade.

In 1766 Josiah Chowning advertised the opening of a tavern where clients could "depend upon the best of entertainment for themselves, servants, and horses, and good pasturage." Josiah Chowning would enjoy the nightly "Gambols" at his tavern, which feature games, ballads, and good food and drink such as barbecued beef ribs, pecan tarts, and mulled apple cider. In the early 1740s, James Shields took over the tavern that his Huguenot father-in-law, John Marot, had operated several decades earlier. Located close to the Capitol, Shields Tavern attracted lower gentry and customers of the "middling sort." Specialties at Shields Tavern today include crayfish soup, spit-roasted meats, and syllabub and other traditional desserts.

Modern dining facilities are also available at Colonial Williamsburg. The menus in the elegant Regency Room and Regency Lounge at the award-winning Williamsburg Inn offer a delectable array of delicious dishes, among them avocados stuffed with crabmeat remoulade and Regency hazelnut ice cream cake. Seafood is featured at the Williamsburg Lodge, where rockfish dijonnaise is a particular favorite. Its beautiful natural setting makes The Cascades the perfect place for a hunt breakfast, a tempting assortment of tidewater specialties.

Breakfast, brunch, luncheon, dinner, or festive holiday celebration—*Favorite Meals from Williamsburg* has a menu and recipes for all tastes and all seasons.

Menus and Recipes

Recipes for starred dishes (*) on each menu are given in this cookbook.

Enlivened by a roving balladeer, Supper and Gambols at Chowning's Tavern features Mulled Apple Cider, Barbecued Beef Ribs, Tossed Salad with Chutney Dressing, and Pecan Tarts. ►

Overleaf:

Individual Two-Egg Omelets are served with a choice of tasty fillings such as Grated Cheddar Cheese, Sliced Mushrooms, Creole Sauce, or Diced Virginia Ham. Above are Blueberry Muffins, Sally Lunn, and Sweet Raisin Bread.

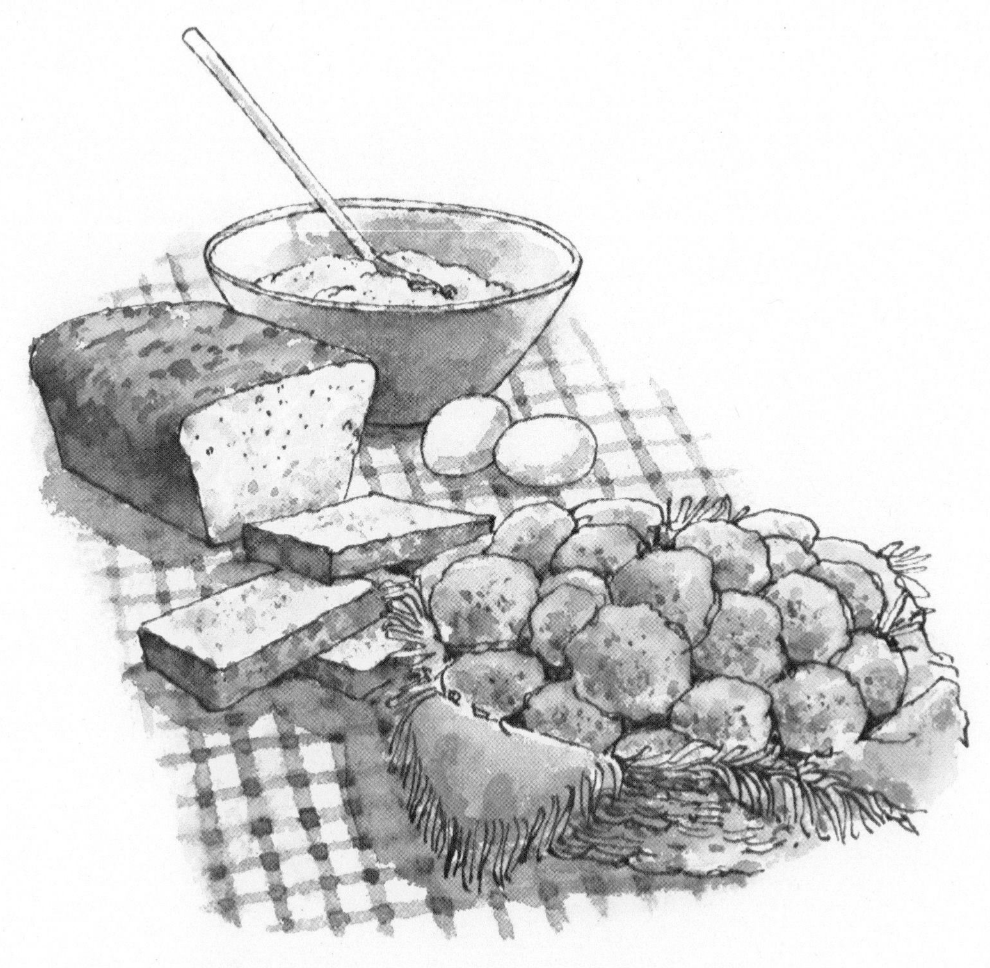

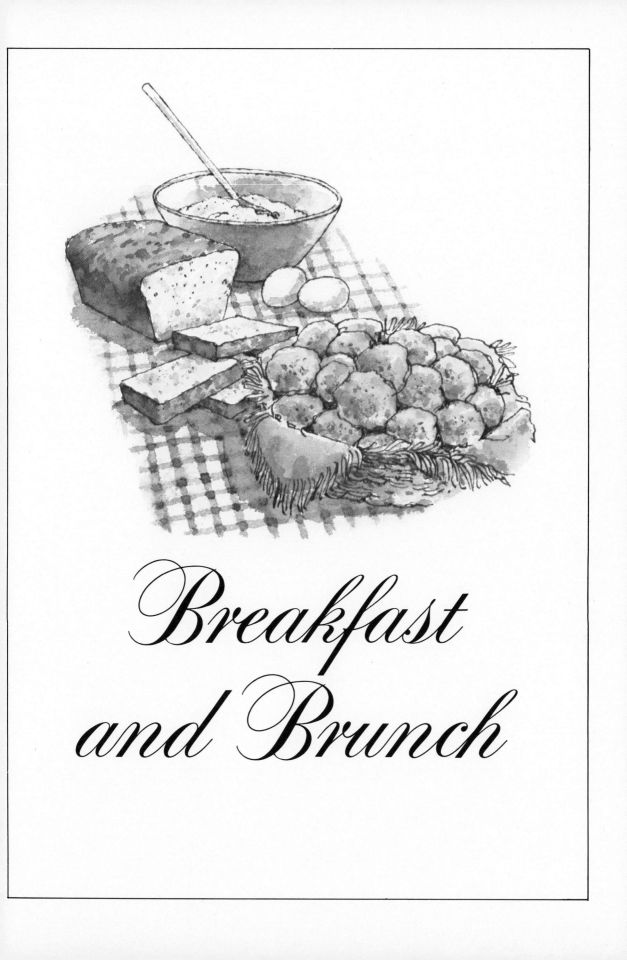

Breakfast and Brunch

The Cascades Hunt Breakfast

for 12

*Tomato Juice Royale

*Scrambled Eggs with Virginia Ham

*Scalloped York River Oysters *or*

*Pan Fried Oysters

*Spicy Cocktail Sauce

*Hashed Brown Potatoes

*Fried Shenandoah Valley Apple Slices

Hominy Grits

*Colonial Buttermilk Biscuits

*Bran Muffins

Coffee, Tea, Milk

Nestled in a beautiful wooded setting complete with waterfall, The Cascades offers delicacies from the Chesapeake Bay country as well as international favorites. It is the perfect place for a hunt breakfast, which features a tempting assortment of tidewater specialties.

TOMATO JUICE ROYALE

(12 servings)

8 cups tomato juice
6 tablespoons lemon juice
2 teaspoons onion juice
1½ teaspoons sugar
1 tablespoon Worcestershire sauce
½ teaspoon Tabasco sauce
4 large fresh basil leaves, chopped, or *1 teaspoon dried basil*
salt
12 small ribs of celery with leaves

Combine the tomato juice, lemon juice, onion juice, sugar, Worcestershire sauce, Tabasco sauce, and basil. Mix well.

Add salt to taste.

Refrigerate overnight.

Strain into a pitcher.

Garnish each serving with a rib of celery.

SCRAMBLED EGGS WITH VIRGINIA HAM

(12 servings)

6 tablespoons butter
24 eggs
1½ cups whipping cream
2½ cups bite-size pieces of VIRGINIA HAM *(page 66)*
1 teaspoon white pepper

Heat the butter in the top of a large double boiler. Spread it around the sides of the pan.

Beat the eggs and cream together until well blended.

Add the Virginia Ham and white pepper.

Cook over hot, not boiling, water, stirring constantly, until the eggs are creamy and lightly scrambled.

Taste for seasoning. Depending on the saltiness of the Virginia Ham, it may be necessary to add a little salt.

SCALLOPED YORK RIVER OYSTERS

(12 servings)

Fried oysters have been popular in Virginia since colonial days, when William Byrd II noted in his diary that "I ate oysters for breakfast." Eighteenth-century cookbooks contain a number recipes for this dish; the ingredients called for and the techniques involved are amazingly modern. Oysters are a delectable addition to The Cascades Hunt Breakfast, and they would be equally delicious at lunch or suppertime.

1½ quarts oysters
4 cups saltine crackers, crumbled
½ teaspoon white pepper
1 cup butter
1½ cups oyster liquor
1 cup light cream
1 tablespoon Worcestershire sauce
½ teaspoon Tabasco sauce
paprika

Preheat the oven to 400° F.

Butter a 13 x 9 x 2-inch casserole.

Drain the oysters, reserving the liquor.

Place the crumbled crackers in a bowl. Add the white pepper. Mix well.

Melt the butter in a large skillet. Add the cracker crumbs and sauté over medium heat until lightly browned. Reserve.

Combine the oyster liquor, cream, Worcestershire sauce, and Tabasco sauce. Mix well. Taste for seasoning.

Spread 1½ cups of crumbs over the bottom of the prepared casserole. Cover with ½ of the oysters. Spoon ½ of the oyster liquor mixture over the oysters. Sprinkle with 1¼ cups of crumbs. Repeat the process. Sprinkle the top layer of crumbs lightly with paprika.

Bake at 400° F. for 25 minutes.

PAN FRIED OYSTERS

(12 servings)

1 quart oysters
2 eggs
2 tablespoons water
¾ cup flour
2 cups fine cracker crumbs
vegetable oil
Spicy Cocktail Sauce *(page 12)*

Line a baking sheet with waxed paper.

Drain the oysters on paper towels.

Beat the eggs and water together until well blended.

Coat each oyster with flour, dip it in the egg mixture, and roll it in the cracker crumbs. Place the oyster on the prepared baking sheet. Repeat the process until all of the oysters have been coated.

Refrigerate, covered with waxed paper, for 2 hours.

Heat ¾ inch of oil to 375° F. in a large deep skillet. Add 6 to 8 oysters and fry for 2 minutes. Turn the oysters over and fry for 1 minute more.

Drain on paper towels.
Serve with Spicy Cocktail Sauce.

SPICY COCKTAIL SAUCE

(1¼ cups)

1 cup catsup
2 tablespoons prepared horseradish
1 teaspoon Worcestershire sauce
2 teaspoons lemon juice
¼ cup celery, finely chopped

Combine the catsup, prepared horseradish, Worcestershire sauce, lemon juice, and celery. Mix well.

Chill thoroughly.

HASHED BROWN POTATOES

(12 servings)

8 cups potatoes, diced
1 tablespoon onion, minced
3 tablespoons parsley, chopped
½ cup butter or *vegetable oil*
salt and freshly ground pepper

Combine the potatoes, onion, and parsley. Mix well.

Heat the butter or oil in a large heavy skillet.

Spread the potato mixture in the skillet, pressing down with a spatula. Cook over medium heat until the bottom is browned.

Carefully turn the potatoes over. Add salt and pepper to taste. Brown on the other side.

FRIED SHENANDOAH VALLEY APPLE SLICES

(12 servings)

12 tart apples
1 cup sugar
1¼ teaspoons cinnamon
1 teaspoon nutmeg
¾ cup butter

Peel and core the apples. Cut them in eighths.

Combine the sugar, cinnamon, and nutmeg. Mix well.

Add the apple slices. Mix well.

Melt the butter in a large deep skillet. Add the apple slices and cook over low heat, stirring occasionally, until done.

Serve hot.

COLONIAL BUTTERMILK BISCUITS

(4 dozen)

2 cups all-purpose flour
2 cups cake flour
½ teaspoon salt
4 teaspoons baking powder
2 tablespoons sugar
½ cup butter
2 egg yolks
1¼ cups buttermilk
melted butter (optional)

Preheat the oven to 450° F.

Lightly grease a baking sheet.

Sift the flours, salt, baking powder, and sugar together.

Cut in the butter with knives or a pastry blender until the mixture is mealy.

Beat the egg yolks and buttermilk together until well blended.

Make a well in the center of the flour mixture. Add the egg yolks and buttermilk. Mix just long enough to moisten completely.

Knead the dough on a lightly floured surface for about 30 seconds. Roll the dough ½ inch thick. Cut the dough with a 1½-inch biscuit cutter.

Brush the tops of the biscuits with melted butter if desired.

Place the biscuits on the prepared baking sheet.

Bake at 450° F. for 12 minutes.

BRAN MUFFINS

(3½ dozen)

1¼ cups milk
1½ cups bran
1 egg
½ cup sugar
½ teaspoon salt
¼ cup molasses
1½ cups all-purpose flour
4 teaspoons baking powder
¼ cup butter, melted

Preheat the oven to 400° F.

Grease muffin tins that are 1½ inches in diameter.

Combine the milk and bran and let stand for 15 minutes.

Beat the egg, sugar, and salt until light and fluffy.

Add the molasses.

Add the bran mixture.

Sift the flour and baking powder together.

Add the dry ingredients, mixing just until blended. Do not overmix.

Add the melted butter.

Spoon into the prepared muffin tins, filling each tin ¾ full.

Bake at 400° F. for 20 minutes.

Special Griddle Cakes Breakfast

for 8

Melon

*Southern Pecan Griddle Cakes *or*

*Blueberry Griddle Cakes

Country Sausage Patties

Coffee

SOUTHERN PECAN GRIDDLE CAKES

(16 griddle cakes)

1 cup all-purpose flour
1 cup cake flour
4 teaspoons baking powder
¼ cup sugar
1 teaspoon salt
2 cups milk
2 eggs
¼ cup butter, melted
1⅓ cups pecans, coarsely chopped
maple syrup

Sift the flours, baking powder, sugar, and salt together.

Beat the milk and eggs until well blended. Add to the flour mixture.

Add the melted butter and pecans, mixing just until blended.

Cook on a lightly greased griddle, using ¼ to ⅓ cup of batter for each griddle cake.

Serve with warm maple syrup.

BLUEBERRY GRIDDLE CAKES

(18–20 griddle cakes)

¾ cup all-purpose flour
¾ cup cake flour
1¾ teaspoons baking powder
3 tablespoons sugar
½ teaspoon salt
1⅓ cups milk
2 eggs, separated
3 tablespoons butter, melted
1 cup fresh blueberries or *frozen blueberries, thawed and drained*
blueberry syrup

Sift the flours, baking powder, sugar, and salt together.

Beat the milk and egg yolks just until blended. Add to the flour mixture, mixing just until blended.

Add the melted butter.

Beat the egg whites until stiff peaks form. Fold the egg whites and blueberries into the batter.

Drop small ladlefuls (3 tablespoons each) of batter onto a lightly greased griddle.

Serve with warm blueberry syrup.

Note: If thawed and drained frozen blueberries are used, do not add the blueberries to the batter. Instead, drop the batter on the griddle and let the first side cook a little. Spoon some berries on top of the batter and let them settle and cook before turning the griddle cake.

Sunday Brunch at The Cascades

for 8

*Frosted Fruit Shrub

*Butter Baked Eggs with Virginia Ham

*Virginia Apple Fritters

*Breakfast Twists *or*

*Colonial Sweet Bread Rings

Coffee

FROSTED FRUIT SHRUB

(8 servings)

3 cups cranberry juice
¾ cup apple juice
1 pint raspberry sherbet
8 mint sprigs

Combine the cranberry and apple juices.
Chill thoroughly.
Top each serving with a scoop of sherbet and stir once or twice.
Garnish with a sprig of mint.

BUTTER BAKED EGGS WITH VIRGINIA HAM

(8 servings)

2 tablespoons butter, melted
1½ cups light cream, divided
1 cup VIRGINIA HAM *(page 66), minced*
2 tablespoons parsley, chopped
Tabasco sauce
16 eggs

Preheat the oven to 400° F.
Brush 8 shirred egg dishes with melted butter.
Pour 1 tablespoon of cream into each dish.
Combine 1 cup of cream with the Virginia Ham, parsley, and 4 drops of Tabasco sauce.
Break 2 eggs into each dish.
Spoon 1 tablespoon of the cream–ham mixture over each egg.
Bake at 400° F. for 10 minutes or until the eggs are set.

VIRGINIA APPLE FRITTERS

(2 dozen)

2 eggs
½ cup sugar
½ teaspoon salt
1½ cups apples, diced
1 cup all-purpose flour
¼ teaspoon baking soda
1 teaspoon baking powder
1 teaspoon cinnamon
½ teaspoon ginger
1 tablespoon butter, melted
1 teaspoon vanilla
vegetable oil
confectioners' sugar

Beat the eggs, sugar, and salt until light and fluffy.
Add the apples. Mix well.
Sift the flour, baking soda, and baking powder together. Add to the egg mixture.
Add the cinnamon, ginger, butter, and vanilla. Mix well.

Refrigerate the batter for at least 2 hours.

Drop by teaspoonfuls into deep hot fat (375° F.) and fry for 3 to 5 minutes. Do not fry more than 4 or 5 fritters at a time.

Drain on paper towels.

Sprinkle with confectioners' sugar before serving.

BREAKFAST TWISTS

(2 loaves)

½ cup lukewarm water
2 packages active dry yeast
1 cup sugar, divided
¼ cup butter
2 eggs
¼ cup powdered milk
½ teaspoon salt
2 cups all-purpose flour
⅔ cup cake flour
1 cup pecans
1½ cups cake crumbs
4 to 5 tablespoons milk
1 egg yolk
1 cup confectioners' sugar
1½ tablespoons boiling water
½ teaspoon vanilla

Preheat the oven to 350° F. 10 minutes before the twists are ready to be baked.

Butter 2 baking sheets.

Combine the water, yeast, and 1 teaspoon of sugar in a bowl. Let proof while proceeding with the recipe.

Cream the butter and ¼ cup of sugar together. Add the eggs, powdered milk, and salt. Beat until smooth.

Add the flours and the yeast mixture. Beat for 5 minutes.

Place the dough in a buttered bowl. Turn the dough around so that it is coated with butter.

Cover the dough and let it rise in a warm, draft-free place (85° F.) until it doubles in bulk.

Process the pecans, cake crumbs, and ¾ cup of sugar in a food processor or blender until smooth. Add enough milk to make a paste.

Roll out the dough into 2 12-inch squares ⅛ inch thick. Spread each square completely with ½ of the filling, smoothing it thinly.

Roll the squares up like a jelly roll. Cut 1 roll in half lengthwise. Turn the cut roll so that 1 end is at the edge of the work surface.

Starting at the midway point, twist 1 half around the other, turning the dough so that the cut side is always uppermost. Squeeze the ends together gently and turn the twist around. Repeat with the other half. Place on the prepared baking sheet.

Repeat with the other roll.

Cover and let the dough rise in a warm, draft-free place for 45 minutes.

Beat the egg yolk and 1 teaspoon of water together until well blended. Brush the twists with the egg glaze.

Bake at 350° F. for 25 minutes.

Combine the confectioners' sugar, boiling water, and vanilla. Beat for 3 minutes.

Spread the icing over the twists while they are still warm.

COLONIAL SWEET BREAD RINGS

(3 rings)

1 cup plus 3 tablespoons lukewarm water, divided
5 packages active dry yeast
⅔ cup sugar, divided
½ cup unsalted butter
1 teaspoon salt
4 eggs
1¾ teaspoons vanilla, divided
6 cups bread flour
1½ cups walnuts, chopped
⅓ cup almonds, sliced
4 ounces candied fruits
3 cups golden raisins
¼ cup butter, melted
1 tablespoon light corn syrup
2 cups confectioners' sugar

Preheat the oven to 375° F. 10 minutes before the rings are ready to be baked.

Lightly butter 3 9-inch round cake pans.

Combine 1 cup of water, the yeast, and 1 teaspoon of sugar in a bowl. Let proof while proceeding with the recipe.

Beat the remaining sugar, butter, and salt until fluffy.

Add the eggs, 1 at a time, beating well after each addition.

Add the yeast mixture and 1½ teaspoons of vanilla.

Gradually add the bread flour, beating constantly. Beat for 5 minutes. Let the dough rest for 20 minutes.

Mix in the nuts, candied fruits, and raisins.

Cover the dough and let it rise in a warm, draft-free place (85° F.) until it doubles in bulk.

Punch the dough down and divide it in thirds. Roll out each third into a rectangle about 14 x 7 inches. Spread the dough with melted butter and roll it up like a jelly roll, starting with the long side.

Coil the roll around a jelly glass that has been brushed with melted butter. Place it in the middle of the prepared pan. Press the ends of the roll together. Repeat with the other 2 portions.

Cover and let the rings rise in a warm, draft-free place until they have increased in bulk about ⅓.

Brush the rings with melted butter.

Bake at 375° F. for 40 minutes.

Combine the corn syrup, 3 tablespoons of water, and ¼ teaspoon of vanilla. Add to the confectioners' sugar, beating until smooth.

Spread the icing over the rings while they are still warm.

Champagne Breakfast for Two at the Williamsburg Inn

for 2

Freshly Squeezed Orange Juice

*Eggs Benedict and Virginia Ham on

*Toasted Sally Lunn

*Hollandaise Sauce

*Pineapple, Peach, and Melon Kabobs

Chilled Champagne

EGGS BENEDICT AND VIRGINIA HAM

(2 servings)

4 slices SALLY LUNN *(below)*
butter
4 thin slices VIRGINIA HAM *(page 66)*
4 eggs
HOLLANDAISE SAUCE *(page 22)*
PINEAPPLE, PEACH, *and* MELON KABOBS *(page 22)*

Toast the Sally Lunn. Butter lightly. Place 2 slices of Sally Lunn on each of 2 warmed plates. Place a slice of Virginia Ham on each piece.

Heat the water for poaching the eggs in a skillet until it simmers. Break the eggs into the simmering water. Poach for 4 to 5 minutes or until the whites are cooked. Transfer the eggs onto the prepared toasts.

Cover the poached eggs with the Hollandaise Sauce.

Garnish with the Pineapple, Peach, and Melon Kabobs.

SALLY LUNN

(2 loaves)

1 cup milk
½ cup vegetable shortening
¼ cup water
4 cups sifted all-purpose flour, divided
⅓ cup sugar
2 teaspoons salt
2 packages active dry yeast
3 eggs

Preheat the oven to 350° F. 10 minutes before the Sally Lunn is ready to be baked.

Butter 2 9¼ x 5¼ x 2¾-inch loaf pans.

Heat the milk, shortening, and water until very warm, about 120° F. The shortening does not need to melt.

Combine 1⅓ cups of flour and the sugar, salt, and yeast in a large mixing bowl.

Add the warm liquids to the flour mixture. Beat with an electric mixer at medium speed for 2 minutes.

Gradually add ⅔ cup of flour and the eggs. Beat at high speed for 2 minutes.

Add 2 cups of flour. Mix well. The batter will be thick but not stiff.

Cover the dough and let it rise in a warm, draft-free place (85° F.) until it doubles in bulk, about 1 to 1¼ hours.

Punch the dough down and divide it between the prepared pans.

Cover and let rise in a warm, draft-free place until it has increased in bulk ⅓ to ½.

Bake at 350° F. for 40 to 50 minutes.

Cool on racks.

HOLLANDAISE SAUCE

(¾ cup)

½ cup butter
2 egg yolks
2 tablespoons cold water
1 tablespoon lemon juice
¼ teaspoon salt
cayenne

Melt the butter slowly. Let it stand for 2 minutes so that the whey will separate from the butter. Pour off and reserve the clear butter. Discard the whey.

Combine the egg yolks and cold water in a stainless steel bowl that will fit over a pan of hot water without letting the water touch the bottom of the bowl.

Whisk the egg yolks until creamy.

When the yolks begin to thicken, gradually add the melted butter, whisking constantly, until all of the butter has been added and the sauce is thick. Remove from the heat.

Add the lemon juice, salt, and a dash of cayenne.

PINEAPPLE, PEACH, AND MELON KABOBS

(2 servings)

1 slice fresh pineapple
1 large peach
1 slice cantaloupe or *honeydew melon*
mint leaves
2 bamboo skewers

Peel the fruit. Cut it into pieces of equal size.

Thread the fruit alternately on the bamboo skewers, interspersing mint leaves in 3 or 4 places.

Chill thoroughly.

Note: Canned fruit may be substituted for the fresh.

Omelet Fare at the Williamsburg Lodge

for 12

Omelets

Individual Two-Egg Omelets with

Sliced Mushrooms

Diced Virginia Ham

Crumbled Crisp Bacon

Grated Cheddar Cheese

Sour Cream and Chives

Baby Shrimp

*Creole Sauce

Fruits

*Hot Fruit Compote *or*

*Baked Apples with

*Rum Custard Sauce

Breads

*Sweet Raisin Bread

*Blueberry Muffins

*Toasted Sally Lunn

The Sunday omelet brunch at the Williamsburg Lodge is enjoyed by visitors to Williamsburg and townspeople alike. Individual two-egg omelets are filled with a variety of tasty ingredients like the ones suggested on the preceding menu—the only limitation is your imagination! Be creative!

CREOLE SAUCE

(3 cups)

¼ cup olive oil
½ cup onion, chopped
½ cup celery, diced
⅓ cup green pepper, chopped
1 clove garlic, minced
1 can (1 pound) plum tomatoes, chopped
½ cup tomato purée
1 small bay leaf
¼ teaspoon thyme
½ teaspoon salt
¼ teaspoon pepper

Heat the oil in a heavy saucepan. Add the onion, celery, green pepper, and garlic and sauté over medium heat until the vegetables are tender. Do not brown.

Add the tomatoes, tomato purée, bay leaf, thyme, salt, and pepper. Bring to a boil, reduce the heat, and simmer, covered, for 1½ hours.

Taste for seasoning.

HOT FRUIT COMPOTE

(12 servings)

2 cans (1 pound each) pears
2 cans (1 pound each) sliced peaches
1 can (15½ ounces) pineapple chunks
24 cooked prunes
3 cups applesauce
1 teaspoon cinnamon
½ teaspoon nutmeg
¼ teaspoon allspice
½ cup brown sugar, packed
¼ cup Grand Marnier

Drain the pears, peaches, and pineapple chunks. Slice the pears.

Purée the cooked prunes in a food processor or blender.

Combine the pears, peaches, pineapple chunks, puréed prunes, and applesauce.

Add the cinnamon, nutmeg, allspice, brown sugar, and Grand Marnier. Mix well.

Cover and let stand at room temperature for several hours. Heat in the top of a double boiler. Serve hot.

BAKED APPLES

(12 servings)

12 baking apples
¼ cup unsalted butter
¼ cup brown sugar
1½ teaspoons cinnamon
¼ cup red currant jelly or *honey*
RUM CUSTARD SAUCE *(below)*

Preheat the oven to 350° F.

Butter a 13 x 9 x 2-inch casserole.

Core the apples. Trim away ½ inch of peel around the stem ends. If the bottoms are uneven, trim them so that the apples will stand upright. Place the apples in the prepared casserole.

Place 1 teaspoon of butter, 1 teaspoon of brown sugar, ⅛ teaspoon of cinnamon, and 1 teaspoon of red currant jelly in the center of each apple.

Bake at 350° F. for 40 to 45 minutes, basting the apples with the pan juices after 20 minutes. The apples should be slightly firm but tender.

Serve with Rum Custard Sauce.

RUM CUSTARD SAUCE

(3 cups)

Colonial cookery books contain instructions for making custards that still pertain today. In *The Experienced English House-keeper*, Mrs. Raffald advised her readers to stir the custard "all one way," to cook it until it "be thick enough," and to keep the mixture from boiling "after the yolks are in."

8 egg yolks
¾ cup sugar
⅛ teaspoon salt
1½ teaspoons vanilla
2 cups milk
½ cup whipping cream
¼ cup white rum

Beat the egg yolks, sugar, salt, and vanilla until light and fluffy.

Scald the milk and cream. Gradually pour over the egg mixture, beating constantly.

Cook over low heat, stirring constantly, until the mixture thickens. Do not let the mixture boil. Remove from the heat.

Cool slightly before adding the rum.

SWEET RAISIN BREAD

(3 loaves)

2 cups lukewarm water
2 packages active dry yeast
3 eggs
½ cup butter
1 tablespoon vanilla, divided
1 teaspoon lemon extract
¾ cup sugar
2 teaspoons salt
7 cups all-purpose flour
1½ cups raisins
1 tablespoon butter, melted
1 cup confectioners' sugar
6 tablespoons milk
2 tablespoons almonds, sliced

Preheat the oven to 375° F. 10 minutes before the bread is ready to be baked.

Grease 3 9¼ x 5¼ x 2¾-inch loaf pans.

Combine the water and yeast in a bowl. Let proof for 3 minutes.

Beat in the eggs, butter, 2 teaspoons of vanilla, and lemon extract until well blended.

Combine the sugar, salt, and flour, add 3 cups to the liquid mixture, and beat for 3 minutes.

Add the remaining flour mixture and beat until well blended.

Add the raisins.

Cover the dough and let it rise in a warm, draft-free place (85° F.) until it doubles in bulk, about 1 to 1¼ hours.

Turn the dough out onto a lightly floured board. Punch it down and cut it in thirds.

Shape the dough into loaves. Place them in the prepared pans. Cover and let rise in a warm, draft-free place for 45 minutes.

Brush the loaves with the melted butter.

Bake at 375° F. for 35 to 40 minutes.

Combine the confectioners' sugar and milk. Beat until smooth. Add 1 teaspoon of vanilla.

Drizzle the glaze over the loaves while they are still warm.

Sprinkle with the sliced almonds.

BLUEBERRY MUFFINS

(1½ dozen)

⅓ cup vegetable shortening
1 cup sugar
2 eggs
1¾ cups all-purpose flour
2 teaspoons baking powder
½ teaspoon salt
⅔ cup milk
1½ cups blueberries
1 tablespoon sugar
2 tablespoons all-purpose flour

Preheat the oven to 400° F.

Grease muffin tins that are 2½ inches in diameter.

Cream the shortening and sugar until light and fluffy. Add the eggs, 1 at a time, beating well after each addition.

Sift the flour, baking powder, and salt together.

Add the dry ingredients and milk alternately, mixing just until blended. Do not overmix.

In a small bowl toss the blueberries with the sugar and flour. Add the blueberries, folding just enough to mix well.

Spoon into the prepared muffin tins, filling each tin ⅔ full. A little sugar and cinnamon may be sprinkled on top of each muffin if desired.

Bake at 400° F. for 20 to 25 minutes.

Note: If frozen blueberries are used, toss gently in a paper towel to remove ice crystals, but do not thaw them.

TOASTED SALLY LUNN

(see page 21)

Luncheon

Summer Luncheon on the Terrace of the Williamsburg Inn

for 4

*Chilled Cream of Asparagus Soup

*Avocados Stuffed with Crabmeat Rémoulade

*Rémoulade Sauce

Hard Rolls

*Caramel Custard

*Caramel Syrup

Guests at the award-winning Williamsburg Inn enjoy distinctive dishes in an atmosphere of quiet elegance. Presidents of the United States, many royal visitors, among them Queen Elizabeth, the Shah of Iran, and Emperor Hirohito, and other international leaders have lodged and dined at the Inn.

CHILLED CREAM OF ASPARAGUS SOUP

(4 servings)

2 cups Chicken Stock *(below)*
or *canned chicken broth*
1 can (15 ounces) asparagus spears, drained
1 small onion, chopped
½ small bay leaf
3 tablespoons butter
3 tablespoons flour
1 cup milk
salt and white pepper
¼ cup whipping cream

Bring the Chicken Stock to a boil. Add the drained asparagus, onion, and bay leaf. Bring to a boil, reduce the heat, and simmer, covered, for 30 minutes. Discard the bay leaf.

Melt the butter in a saucepan. Stir in the flour and cook over medium heat for 3 minutes, stirring constantly. Do not let the mixture brown.

Heat the milk and add it to the butter and flour mixture, whisking until the mixture is smooth and thick.

Purée the asparagus–Chicken Stock mixture in a food processor or blender. Strain through a sieve into the milk mixture, pressing down hard on the solids with the back of a wooden spoon. Cook over medium heat, whisking constantly, until the mixture is slightly thickened.

Add salt and white pepper to taste.

Chill thoroughly.

Taste for seasoning after the soup is chilled.

Stir in the cream just before serving.

CHICKEN STOCK

(4 quarts)

½ teaspoon thyme
1 bay leaf
½ teaspoon marjoram
3 sprigs parsley
6 peppercorns
2 onions, sliced
salt
3 ribs of celery with leaves, sliced
3 carrots, sliced
2 leeks, sliced
5 pounds chicken necks, backs, and wings

Tie the thyme, bay leaf, marjoram, parsley, and peppercorns in a cheesecloth bag. Place in a soup pot.

Add the onions, celery, carrots, leeks, and chicken.

Cover with cold water. Bring to a boil, reduce the heat, and simmer, partially covered, for 2 to 3 hours or until the chicken comes easily from the bones. Remove the chicken.

Simmer, uncovered, until the stock is reduced to 4 quarts. Add salt to taste.

Refrigerate. Strain the stock and remove all fat.

Note: Stock can be frozen for future use.

AVOCADOS STUFFED WITH CRABMEAT RÉMOULADE

(4 servings)

12 ounces backfin crabmeat
1 tablespoon lemon juice
RÉMOULADE SAUCE *(below)*
2 large avocados
lettuce
tomato wedges
lemon wedges
black olives

Pick over the crabmeat. Discard any bits of shell or cartilage.

Toss the crabmeat gently with the lemon juice. Gently fold in the Remoulade Sauce.

Peel the avocados, halve them, and remove the seeds.

Arrange lettuce leaves on each of 4 plates. Place an avocado half on each plate. Fill the center with the crabmeat mixture.

Garnish with tomato and lemon wedges and black olives.

RÉMOULADE SAUCE

(¾ cup)

1 teaspoon capers, finely chopped
1 teaspoon gherkins, finely chopped
½ teaspoon fresh tarragon, finely chopped
1 anchovy fillet, finely chopped
¾ teaspoon Dijon mustard
¾ cup MAYONNAISE *(page 43)*

Combine the capers, gherkins, tarragon, and anchovy fillet.

Add the mustard and Mayonnaise. Mix well.

Chill thoroughly.

CARAMEL CUSTARD

(4–5 servings)

2 eggs
2 egg yolks
⅓ cup sugar
2 cups milk
⅛ teaspoon salt
¾ teaspoon vanilla
CARAMEL SYRUP *(below)*

Preheat the oven to 350° F.

Beat the eggs and egg yolks. Gradually add the sugar and beat until the mixture is light and fluffy.

Scald the milk. Gradually pour it over the egg mixture, beating constantly.

Add the salt and vanilla.

Pour into individual custard cups or ovenproof glass dishes.

Place in a roasting pan. Fill the pan with enough hot water to come ⅔ of the way up the sides of the dishes.

Bake at 350° F. for 30 minutes or until the custard tests done.

Remove from the water bath.

Cool on a rack.

Just before serving, run a knife around the edge of the custards and invert into sherbet or champagne glasses.

Pour cold Caramel Syrup over the custards.

CARAMEL SYRUP

(½ cup)

½ cup sugar
¼ cup cold water
½ cup boiling water

Combine the sugar and cold water in a heavy saucepan. Swirl the mixture until the sugar dissolves. Do not stir.

Add the boiling water. Boil over medium heat, without stirring, until the syrup is the color of butterscotch. Remove from the heat.

Cool.

Refrigerate.

Note: The syrup will thicken as it cools.

A Hearty Luncheon at King's Arms Tavern

for 6

*Leek and Potato Soup

*Yorkshire Meat Pies with

*Yorkshire Topping

*Mushroom Sauce

*King's Arms Salad

*Red Wine Vinegar Dressing

*Mrs. Randolph's Frozen Lemonade

Located on historic Duke of Gloucester Street, the King's Arms Tavern was one of Williamsburg's most genteel hostelries in the eighteenth century. Its select clientele included Burgesses and Councillors like George Washington, Sir Peyton Skipwith, and William Byrd III. Today, paneling and handsome furnishings of eighteenth-century design lend the King's Arms an air of hospitality and comfort. Luncheon or dinner at the King's Arms Tavern is always a memorable experience.

LEEK AND POTATO SOUP

(6 servings)

4 cups Chicken Stock *(page 30)* or *canned chicken broth*
1 cup potatoes, diced
1 medium onion, diced
1 leek, diced
¼ cup butter
3 tablespoons flour
2 cups milk
salt and white pepper

Bring the Chicken Stock to a boil. Add the potatoes, onion, and leek. Reduce the heat and simmer, covered, until the vegetables are tender.

Melt the butter in a saucepan. Stir in the flour and cook over low heat for 3 minutes, stirring constantly. Do not let the mixture brown.

Heat the milk and add it to the butter and flour mixture, whisking until the mixture is smooth and slightly thickened.

Add the stock and vegetables.

Add salt and white pepper to taste.

YORKSHIRE MEAT PIES

(6 servings)

1 package (10 ounces) frozen mixed vegetables
1 pound ground chuck
2 tablespoons butter
2 tablespoons onion, finely chopped
2 tablespoons flour
2 cups Beef Stock *(page 35)* or *canned beef bouillon*
¼ cup red wine
1 teaspoon tomato paste
salt and pepper
Yorkshire Topping *(page 36)*
parsley
Mushroom Sauce *(page 36)*

Preheat the oven to 400° F. 10 minutes before the meat pies are ready to be baked.

Butter 6 individual casseroles or shirred egg dishes.

Thaw and drain the frozen vegetables.

Sauté the ground chuck in a heavy skillet over medium heat until it is well browned. Drain. Reserve.

Melt the butter in a heavy saucepan. Add the onion and sauté over medium heat until soft. Add the beef. Stir in the flour and cook until it disappears.

Add the Beef Stock, wine, and tomato paste. Simmer, partially covered, for 1 hour or until the mixture is very moist but most of the liquid has reduced.

Add salt and pepper to taste.

Increase the heat to medium, add the thawed and drained mixed vegetables, and heat briefly.

Place in the prepared casseroles.

Bake at 400° F. for 5 minutes. Remove from the oven.

Beat the Yorkshire Topping briefly and pour over the meat mixture.

Return the casseroles to the oven and bake at 400° F. for 25 to 35 minutes or until the Yorkshire Topping is puffy and golden.

Garnish with parsley.

Serve with Mushroom Sauce.

Note: 2 cups of any kind of cooked vegetables may be substituted for the mixed vegetables.

BEEF STOCK

(4–5 quarts)

10 pounds beef bones
¼ cup vegetable oil
3 medium onions, chopped
2 ribs of celery, chopped
2 carrots, chopped
2 cloves garlic, minced
1½ cups whole canned tomatoes
½ cup tomato purée
½ teaspoon thyme
½ teaspoon pepper
1 bay leaf

Preheat the oven to 400° F.

Saw the beef bones in half or ask the butcher to do it. Place the bones in a roasting pan and brown in the oven at 400° F. for 45 minutes or until well browned.

Remove from the oven, drain the fat, and place the bones in a soup pot.

Heat the oil in a heavy skillet. Add the onions, celery, carrots, and garlic. Brown well. Drain.

Add the browned vegetables, tomatoes, tomato purée, thyme, pepper, and bay leaf to the pot of bones.

Cover with cold water. Bring to a boil, reduce the heat, and simmer, uncovered, for 6 to 8 hours, removing any scum that appears on the surface.

Strain the stock and remove all fat.

Refrigerate.

Note: Stock can be frozen for future use.

YORKSHIRE TOPPING

(6 servings)

3 eggs
1 cup milk
1 cup all-purpose flour
¼ teaspoon salt
1 tablespoon butter, melted

Beat the eggs until light. Add the milk, flour, and salt. Beat until smooth.

Add the melted butter.

Cover and let stand at room temperature for at least 30 minutes.

MUSHROOM SAUCE

(1½ cups)

3 tablespoons butter, divided
½ cup fresh mushrooms, sliced
1 tablespoon onion, finely chopped
1 teaspoon parsley, minced
2 tablespoons flour
1½ cups BEEF STOCK *(page 35)* or *canned beef bouillon*
1 to 2 tablespoons red wine
salt and pepper

Melt 1 tablespoon of butter in a small skillet. Add the mushrooms and sauté over medium heat for 2 minutes. Reserve.

Melt 2 tablespoons of butter in a heavy saucepan. Add the onion and parsley and sauté over medium heat until the onion is soft. Do not brown.

Stir in the flour. Cook over medium heat for 3 to 4 minutes, stirring constantly.

Heat the Beef Stock and add it to the mixture, whisking until the mixture is smooth and thick. Add 1 to 2 tablespoons of red wine and salt and pepper to taste. Cook for 5 minutes or until slightly thickened.

Add the sautéed mushrooms.

KING'S ARMS SALAD

(6 servings)

1 small head iceberg lettuce
1 bunch watercress
2 cups red cabbage, shredded
RED WINE VINEGAR DRESSING *(below)*
2 tablespoons chives, chopped

Tear the lettuce into small pieces.

Remove the stem ends from the watercress.

Toss the lettuce, watercress, and cabbage with the Red Wine Vinegar Dressing.

Garnish with the chives.

RED WINE VINEGAR DRESSING

(1⅓ cups)

½ teaspoon salt
⅛ teaspoon pepper
1 teaspoon Dijon mustard
⅓ cup red wine vinegar
⅓ cup olive oil
⅔ cup vegetable oil

Combine the salt, pepper, and mustard. Add the vinegar. Mix well.

Add the oils slowly, whisking constantly.

MRS. RANDOLPH'S FROZEN LEMONADE

(2 quarts)

2 cups sugar
6 cups water
1 cup light corn syrup
2 cans (6 ounces each) frozen lemonade concentrate
rind of 2 lemons, grated

Combine the sugar and water in a saucepan. Bring to a boil and boil, uncovered, for 5 minutes. Remove from the heat.

Add the corn syrup, frozen lemonade concentrate, and grated lemon rind.

Cool completely.

Strain the mixture into the freezer container of an electric ice cream maker.

Follow the manufacturer's directions for freezing.

Cascades Soup and Sandwich Lunch

for 4

*Zucchini and Summer Squash Soup

*Crab Rolls

*Lemon Meringue Pie

ZUCCHINI AND SUMMER SQUASH SOUP

(4 servings)

1 pound small zucchini
1 pound small summer squash
¼ cup butter
¼ cup shallot, minced
2 cups CHICKEN STOCK *(page 30)* or *canned chicken broth*
⅔ cup whipping cream
salt and white pepper

Wash and trim the zucchini and summer squash but do not peel them. Reserve 4 thin slices off the tip end of 1 zucchini and 1 summer squash for garnish.

Slice the rest of the squash in ½-inch pieces.

Melt the butter in a saucepan. Add the shallot and squash and sauté over medium heat for 5 minutes. Do not brown.

Add the Chicken Stock and simmer for 10 minutes or until the squash is tender.

Drain the squash, reserving the liquid. Purée the squash in a food processor or blender. Combine the puréed squash with the reserved liquid.

Return to the heat and add the cream. Do not boil.

Add salt and white pepper to taste.

Garnish with the reserved slices of zucchini and summer squash.

CRAB ROLLS

(4 servings)

4 hamburger rolls
½ pound crabmeat
2 tablespoons celery, minced
Tabasco sauce
Worcestershire sauce
3 tablespoons MAYONNAISE *(page 43)*
lettuce
8 strips pimiento
4 dill pickles

Toast the hamburger rolls.

Pick over the crabmeat. Discard any bits of shell or cartilage.

Combine the crabmeat, celery, 3 to 4 drops of Tabasco sauce, and 2 drops of Worcestershire sauce. Add the Mayonnaise.

Place a leaf of lettuce on each roll. Divide the crabmeat mixture among the rolls.

Garnish with pimiento strips and a dill pickle.

LEMON MERINGUE PIE

1¾ cups sugar, divided
½ cup cornstarch
½ teaspoon salt, divided
1½ cups water
3 eggs, separated
⅓ cup lemon juice
5 teaspoons lemon rind, grated
2 tablespoons butter
1 9-inch baked PIE SHELL *(page 40)*

Preheat the oven to 350° F. 10 minutes before the meringue is ready to be browned.

Reserve 6 tablespoons of sugar for the meringue.

Combine the remaining sugar with the cornstarch and ¼ teaspoon of salt in a saucepan. Add the water. Stir until the sugar and cornstarch dissolve. Cook over medium heat, stirring constantly, for 3 minutes or until the mixture is smooth and almost transparent. Remove from the heat.

Beat the egg yolks and lemon juice together. Add a little of the hot mixture, stirring constantly.

Pour the egg yolk mixture into the saucepan and cook, stirring constantly, until thick. Remove from the heat.

Add the lemon rind and butter. Mix well.

Place plastic wrap directly on the surface of the lemon filling to prevent a film from forming while it cools. Cool completely.

When the filling is cold, spoon it into the Pie Shell.

Beat the egg whites and ¼ teaspoon of salt until soft peaks form. Gradually add 6 tablespoons of sugar and beat until stiff peaks form.

Pile the meringue on top of the filling. Spread the meringue to the edges of the crust to seal and prevent shrinking.

Bake at 350° F. for 12 to 15 minutes or until the meringue is lightly browned.

Cool the pie on a rack for at least 2 hours before cutting it.

PIE SHELL

(one 9-inch shell)

1 cup all-purpose flour
¼ teaspoon salt
½ teaspoon sugar
¼ cup vegetable shortening
2 tablespoons lard
3 tablespoons ice water

Preheat the oven to 425° F. 10 minutes before the shell is ready to be baked.

Lightly oil a 9-inch pie pan.

Combine the flour, salt, and sugar. Mix well.

Cut in the shortening and lard with knives or a pastry blender until the mixture is mealy. Stir the ice water into the flour mixture. Mix well.

Wrap the dough in waxed paper. Refrigerate for 30 minutes.

Roll out the dough ⅛ inch thick on a lightly floured board or pastry cloth. Press it firmly into the prepared pan. Prick the dough well with a fork.

Bake at 425° F. for 12 to 15 minutes or until golden brown.

Cool the pie shell completely before filling it.

Chowning's Tavern Midday Fare

for 6

*Plantation Vegetable and Beef Soup

*Sippets

*Chowning's Chicken Salad

*French Dressing

*Mayonnaise

*Orange Nut Pound Cake with Vanilla Ice Cream

PLANTATION VEGETABLE AND BEEF SOUP

(6 servings)

¼ cup vegetable oil
2 medium onions, chopped
2 carrots, chopped
1½ cups celery, diced
8 cups CHICKEN STOCK *(page 30)* or *canned chicken broth*
1 cup plum tomatoes, drained and chopped
6 ounces lean beef, diced
salt and pepper
½ cup peas, cooked
SIPPETS *(below)*

Heat the oil in a heavy saucepan. Add the onions, carrots, and celery and sauté over medium heat until the vegetables are tender. Do not brown.

Add the Chicken Stock and tomatoes. Bring to a boil, reduce the heat, and simmer, uncovered, for 30 minutes, removing any scum that appears on the surface.

Add the meat and salt and pepper to taste and simmer for 10 minutes.

Add the peas just before serving.

Serve with Sippets.

SIPPETS

(6 servings)

Since the seventeenth century the term "sippets" has described strips of toast used to sop up soup or broth. In *The Compleat Housewife*, Mrs. E. Smith instructed the home cook who followed her recipe for a "Ragoo of Oysters" to "serve it up with sippets."

Trim the crusts from 6 ½-inch thick slices of Sally Lunn or other firm white bread. Cut each slice into 4 horizontal strips.

Brown the sippets in the oven or toast lightly.

CHOWNING'S CHICKEN SALAD

(6 servings)

3 cups cooked chicken, coarsely diced
½ cup celery, minced
¼ cup FRENCH DRESSING *(page 43)*
2 tablespoons lemon juice
Tabasco sauce
salt
MAYONNAISE *(page 43)*
lettuce
6 hard-cooked eggs, quartered
6 black olives
6 tablespoons sliced almonds, toasted

Combine the chicken, celery, French Dressing, lemon juice, and 4 to 6 drops of Tabasco sauce. Add salt to taste. Mix well.

Chill thoroughly.

Just before serving, add the Mayonnaise.

Arrange lettuce leaves on each of 6 plates.

Divide the salad among the plates.

Garnish with the hard-cooked egg quarters and black olives. Sprinkle each salad with 1 tablespoon of the almonds.

FRENCH DRESSING

(1 cup)

1 teaspoon salt
½ teaspoon freshly ground pepper
¾ teaspoon dry mustard
¼ cup wine vinegar
6 tablespoons olive oil
6 tablespoons vegetable oil

Combine the salt, pepper, and mustard. Add the vinegar. Cover and allow to steep for a few minutes.

Add the oils slowly, whisking constantly.

MAYONNAISE

(1¼ cups)

2 egg yolks
½ teaspoon Dijon mustard
½ teaspoon salt
⅛ teaspoon white pepper
½ cup vegetable oil
½ cup olive oil
2 tablespoons white wine vinegar or *lemon juice*

The egg yolks, oils, and bowl should be at room temperature.

Whisk the egg yolks, mustard, salt, and white pepper together in a small bowl.

Add the oils slowly, whisking constantly, until the mayonnaise begins to emulsify.

When the mayonnaise has thickened, add the vinegar or lemon juice alternately with the last of the oil.

ORANGE NUT POUND CAKE

1 cup butter
1½ teaspoons orange rind, grated
½ teaspoon lemon rind, grated
1 cup sugar
5 eggs
¼ teaspoon orange extract
2 cups all-purpose flour
½ teaspoon baking powder
½ cup pecans, chopped
vanilla ice cream

Grease well and lightly flour a 9¼ x 5¼ x 2¾-inch loaf pan.

All of the ingredients should be at room temperature.

Cream the butter and orange and lemon rinds. Gradually add the sugar. Beat the mixture until it is light and fluffy.

Add the eggs, 1 at a time, beating well after each addition. Add the orange extract.

Sift the flour and baking powder together. Gradually add to the egg mixture.

Add the pecans.

Spoon into the prepared pan.

Place the pan in a cold oven. Turn the oven on to 325° F. and bake for 70 minutes or until done.

Cool in the pan for 10 minutes before turning out onto a rack.

Serve with vanilla ice cream.

A Hearty Luncheon at King's Arms Tavern includes Yorkshire Meat Pie with Yorkshire Topping and Mushroom Sauce, King's Arms Salad, and Mrs. Randolph's Frozen Lemonade. ►

Overleaf:
A beautiful wooded setting complete with waterfall makes The Cascades the perfect site for a refreshing lunch of Zucchini and Summer Squash Soup and Crab Rolls.

The Williamsburg Lodge Special Luncheon

for 8

*Cream of Broccoli Soup

*Chicken Tetrazzini

Lodge Garden Salad

*French Dressing

*Blueberry Crisp with Heavy Cream

CREAM OF BROCCOLI SOUP

(8 servings)

3 tablespoons butter
¾ cup onion, chopped
3 cups potatoes, diced
¼ teaspoon curry powder
1 cup water
1 package (10 ounces) frozen broccoli, thawed
2½ cups Chicken Stock *(page 30)* or *canned chicken broth*
2½ cups milk, divided
¾ cup whipping cream
⅛ teaspoon nutmeg
salt and white pepper

Melt the butter in a saucepan. Add the onion, potatoes, curry powder, and water. Simmer, covered, over medium heat until the vegetables are tender.

Purée the thawed broccoli and the Chicken Stock in a food processor or blender. Pour into the top of a double boiler.

Purée the potato mixture with 1½ cups of milk and pour into the top of the double boiler.

Add 1 cup of milk and the cream and nutmeg. Add salt and white pepper to taste.

Heat over boiling water until very hot but do not boil.

CHICKEN TETRAZZINI

(8 servings)

4 chicken breasts, skinned and boned
½ cup butter, divided
1 onion, chopped
1 carrot, chopped
1 rib celery, thinly sliced
2 cups Chicken Stock *(page 30)* or *canned chicken broth*
½ cup water
1 sprig parsley
½ bay leaf
½ teaspoon salt
⅛ teaspoon white pepper
½ pound mushrooms, thinly sliced
¼ cup flour
1 egg yolk
½ cup whipping cream
¼ cup sherry
¾ pound thin spaghetti
½ cup Parmesan cheese, grated

Preheat the oven to 400° F. 10 minutes before the tetrazzini are ready to go in.

Butter 8 individual casseroles.

Pound the chicken breasts between 2 pieces of waxed paper until flat.

Melt 2 tablespoons of butter in a saucepan. Add the onion, carrot, and celery and sauté over medium heat until the onion is soft. Do not brown.

Add the Chicken Stock, water, parsley, bay leaf, salt, and white pepper. Bring to a boil, reduce the heat, and simmer, covered, for 20 minutes.

Add the chicken breasts and simmer, covered, for 20 minutes or until the chicken is tender.

Remove the chicken from the stock. When it is cool enough to handle, cut the chicken into thin strips.

Strain the stock and remove all fat.

Melt 1 tablespoon of butter in a skillet. Add the mushrooms and sauté over medium heat until they are almost dry. Reserve.

Melt 4 tablespoons of butter in a saucepan. Stir in the flour and cook over medium heat for 3 minutes, stirring constantly. Do not let the mixture brown.

Heat 2 cups of the stock and add it to the mixture, whisking until the mixture is smooth and thick.

Beat the egg yolk and cream together until well blended. Add a little of the hot sauce, stirring constantly. Pour the cream mixture into the saucepan and cook, whisking constantly, until the mixture is almost to the boiling point. Remove from the heat.

Add the chicken, mushrooms, and sherry. Taste for seasoning.

Cook the spaghetti in boiling salted water until tender. Drain. Rinse with hot water.

Arrange a ring of spaghetti in each of the prepared casseroles. Fill the centers with the chicken mixture.

Sprinkle the casseroles with Parmesan. Dot with the remaining tablespoon of butter.

Bake at 400° F. for 15 minutes or until bubbly. Brown quickly under the broiler.

FRENCH DRESSING

(see page 43)

BLUEBERRY CRISP

(8 servings)

2 cans (17 ounces each) blueberries in heavy syrup
½ cup sugar
¼ cup cornstarch
⅛ teaspoon cinnamon
1 tablespoon lemon juice
¾ cup butter
1 cup dark brown sugar
1 cup all-purpose flour
¼ teaspoon salt
¾ cup cornflake crumbs
¾ cup pecans, coarsely chopped
heavy cream

Preheat the oven to 400° F.

Butter a 13 x 9 x 2-inch casserole.

Drain the blueberries, reserving ¾ cup of the syrup.

Combine the sugar, cornstarch, cinnamon, lemon juice, and blueberry syrup in a saucepan. Stir until the sugar and cornstarch dissolve. Cook over medium heat, stirring constantly, until the mixture is thick and almost transparent. Remove from the heat.

Add the blueberries. Cool.

Cream the butter and brown sugar until light and fluffy.

Sift the flour and salt into the mixture. Mix well.

Add the cornflake crumbs and pecans. Mix well.

Spread ½ of the crumb–nut mixture over the bottom of the prepared casserole. Pat it firmly to form a bottom crust.

Pour in the blueberry filling.

Crumble the remaining crumb–nut mixture over the blueberry filling.

Bake at 400° F. for 30 minutes.

Serve with heavy cream.

A Family Tavern Treat

for 8

*Captain Rasmussen's Clam Chowder

*Minced Virginia Ham Sandwiches

*Sally Lunn Rolls

*Tavern Relish

*Lime Sherbet

CAPTAIN RASMUSSEN'S CLAM CHOWDER

(8 servings)

12 chowder clams
4 cups water
¼ cup butter
1 cup onion, chopped
¾ cup celery, diced
¾ cup carrot, diced
½ cup green pepper, diced
1 clove garlic, pressed
½ cup plum tomatoes, chopped
¼ cup tomato purée
1 cup potatoes, cubed
⅛ teaspoon rosemary
⅛ teaspoon thyme
½ teaspoon salt
⅛ teaspoon white pepper
¼ teaspoon pepper

Scrub the clams well. Steam them in 4 cups of water.

Remove the clams from their shells. Chop the clams finely. Reserve.

Strain the clam broth. Reserve.

Melt the butter in a large saucepan. Add the onion, celery, carrot, and green pepper and sauté over medium heat until the vegetables are tender. Do not brown.

Add the garlic, tomatoes, tomato purée, potatoes, rosemary, thyme, salt, white and black pepper, and clam broth. Bring to a boil, reduce the heat, and simmer, covered, for 20 minutes.

Taste for seasoning.

Add the chopped clams. Heat almost to the boiling point.

Note: If fresh clams are not available, 1 bottle (8 ounces) clam juice and 2 cans (6½ ounces each) minced clams and their liquid may be substituted.

MINCED VIRGINIA HAM SANDWICHES

(8 servings)

2 cups Virginia Ham *(page 66), minced, well packed*
2 tablespoons onion, minced
4 teaspoons Tavern Relish *(page 51)*
½ cup Mayonnaise *(page 43)*
2 teaspoons Dijon mustard
¼ teaspoon pepper
8 Sally Lunn Rolls *(page 51)*
butter
lettuce
4 hard-cooked eggs, halved
black olives
tomato wedges

Combine the Virginia Ham, onion, Tavern Relish, Mayonnaise, mustard, and pepper. Mix well.

Chill thoroughly.

Butter the Sally Lunn Rolls. Place a leaf of lettuce on each. Divide the ham mixture among the rolls.

Garnish with the hard-cooked egg halves, black olives, and tomato wedges.

SALLY LUNN ROLLS

(1 dozen)

Preheat the oven to 400° F. 10 minutes before the rolls are ready to be baked.

Follow the directions for Sally Lunn (page 21), increasing the amount of flour to 4⅔ cups.

Shape the rolls with floured hands, tucking the edges under to form round domes.

Place the rolls 4 inches apart on lightly greased baking sheets.

Cover and let rise in a warm, draft-free place (85° F.) for 45 minutes.

Bake at 400° F. for 20 minutes.

TAVERN RELISH

(3 8-ounce jars)

4 cups green tomatoes, chopped
1 tablespoon pickling salt
2 cups cabbage, shredded
1 cup cider vinegar
1 cup sugar
⅓ cup onion, chopped
⅓ cup green pepper, minced
½ cup sweet red pepper, minced
½ teaspoon celery seed
½ teaspoon mustard seed
½ teaspoon cardamom seed
6 peppercorns
½ teaspoon cloves
½ teaspoon cinnamon

Combine the tomatoes and salt. Cover and let stand in a cool place overnight.

Drain the tomatoes. Combine the tomatoes, cabbage, and vinegar in a saucepan. Bring to a boil, reduce the heat, and simmer, uncovered, for 30 minutes.

Add the sugar, onion, green pepper, red pepper, celery seed, mustard seed, cardamom seed, peppercorns, cloves, and cinnamon. Mix well. Bring to a boil, reduce the heat, and simmer, uncovered, until the mixture thickens.

Pour the relish into 3 8-ounce sterilized jars. Seal immediately.

Store in a cool place.

LIME SHERBET

(1½ quarts)

1½ cups sugar
½ cup lime juice
1 teaspoon lime rind, grated
4 cups milk
green food coloring

Combine the sugar and lime juice. Stir until the sugar dissolves.

Add the lime rind, milk, and a few drops of food coloring.

Strain the mixture into the freezer container of an electric ice cream maker.

Follow the manufacturer's directions for freezing.

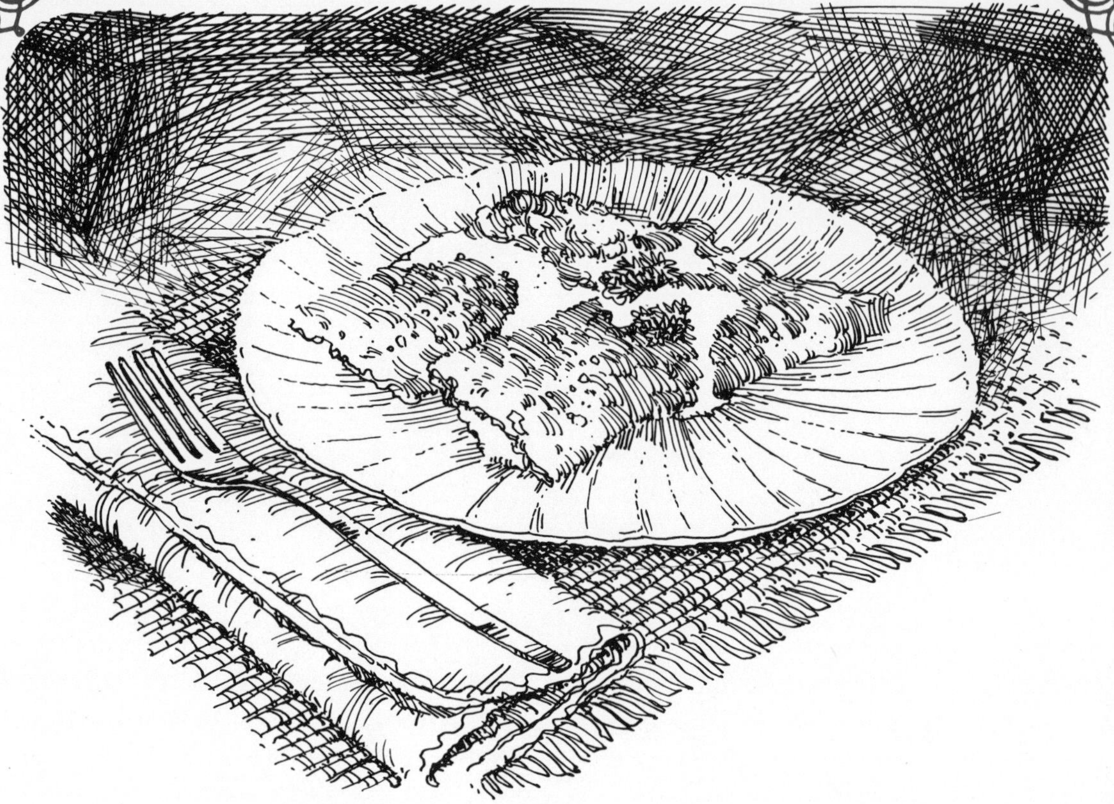

Quiche or Crêpes at The Cascades

for 8

*Quiche Virginian *or*

*Creamed Chicken Crêpes

*Mornay Sauce

*Citrus Fruit Garnish

*Poppy Seed–Honey Dressing

*Strawberry Cake

QUICHE VIRGINIAN

(8 servings)

PASTRY *(below)*
1 cup VIRGINIA HAM *(page 66), diced*
¾ cup Parmesan cheese, grated
1 tablespoon chives, chopped
1½ cups Swiss cheese, grated
4 eggs
2 cups light cream
¼ teaspoon white pepper
⅛ teaspoon nutmeg
CITRUS FRUIT GARNISH *(page 55)*

Preheat the oven to 400° F.

Lightly oil a 10-inch quiche dish or pie pan.

Roll out the Pastry ⅛ inch thick on a lightly floured board or pastry cloth. Press it firmly into the prepared dish. Prick the dough well with a fork.

Bake at 400° F. for 5 minutes. Cool.

Reduce the heat to 350° F.

Combine the Virginia Ham, Parmesan, and chives.

Cover the bottom of the shell with the Swiss cheese. Spread the ham mixture over the cheese.

Beat the eggs, cream, white pepper, and nutmeg together until well blended. Taste for seasoning. Depending on the saltiness of the Virginia Ham, it may be necessary to add a little salt.

Pour the mixture into the shell.

Bake at 350° F. for 40 minutes or until done.

Let the quiche stand for 10 minutes before cutting it.

Garnish with Citrus Fruit Garnish.

PASTRY

(one 10-inch shell)

1½ cups all-purpose flour
½ teaspoon salt
¼ cup vegetable shortening
¼ cup lard
¼ cup ice water

Combine the flour and salt. Mix well.

Cut in the shortening and lard with knives or a pastry blender until the mixture is mealy. Stir the ice water into the flour mixture. Mix well.

Wrap the dough in waxed paper. Refrigerate for 30 minutes.

◄ *Christiana Campbell's Tavern is noted for its Chesapeake Bay Jambalaya, a savory combination of oysters and shrimp.*

Overleaf:
Chilled Cucumber Soup with Tarragon, Colonial Buttermilk Biscuits with Minced Virginia Ham, Pâté Maison, Shrimp Tomatoes, Strawberries Marinated in Grand Marnier, and Lace Cookies make a delightful Picnic on the James River.

CREAMED CHICKEN CRÊPES

(8 servings)

6 tablespoons butter
6 tablespoons flour
1 cup milk
½ cup Chicken Stock *(page 30)* or *canned chicken broth*
½ cup white wine
3 cups cooked chicken, diced
½ cup pecan halves
½ cup pineapple chunks
salt and white pepper
16 cooked Crêpes *(below)*
Mornay Sauce *(page 55)*
¼ cup pecans, finely chopped
Citrus Fruit Garnish *(page 55)*

Preheat the oven to 400° F.

Butter a large ovenproof casserole.

Melt the butter in a saucepan. Stir in the flour and cook over low heat for 3 minutes, stirring constantly. Do not let the mixture brown.

Heat the milk and Chicken Stock and add to the mixture, whisking until the mixture is smooth and thick. Remove from the heat.

Add the wine, chicken, pecan halves, and pineapple.

Add salt and white pepper to taste.

Fill the cooked crêpes with the creamed chicken mixture. Place the crêpes, seam side down, in the prepared casserole. Top each crêpe with Mornay Sauce. Sprinkle with the chopped pecans.

Bake at 400° F. for 10 minutes. Brown quickly under the broiler.

Serve on individual warmed plates.

Garnish with Citrus Fruit Garnish.

CRÊPE BATTER

(8 servings)

1½ cups all-purpose flour
⅛ teaspoon salt
3 eggs
1½ cups milk
3 tablespoons butter, melted
vegetable oil

Place the flour, salt, eggs, milk, and melted butter in the container of a food processor or blender. Process for 1 minute. Scrape down the sides and process for 5 seconds longer.

Refrigerate the batter for at least 2 hours.

Heat a crêpe pan to medium hot. Brush it lightly with oil. Swirling and tipping the pan, pour in just enough batter so that the bottom is entirely covered. Pour any excess batter back into the bowl.

As soon as the top of the crêpe is covered with tiny holes, turn it over and cook for about 30 seconds on the other side. Place the cooked crêpe on a waxed paper covered surface.

Repeat the process until all of the batter has been used.

MORNAY SAUCE

(1½ cups)

¼ cup butter
¼ cup flour
1 cup milk
½ cup CHICKEN STOCK *(page 30)* or *canned chicken broth*
1 egg yolk
2 tablespoons whipping cream
3 tablespoons Parmesan cheese, grated
salt and white pepper

Melt the butter in a saucepan. Stir in the flour and cook over low heat for 3 minutes, stirring constantly. Do not let the mixture brown.

Heat the milk and Chicken Stock and add to the mixture, whisking until the mixture is smooth and thick.

Beat the egg yolk and cream together until well blended. Add a little of the hot sauce, stirring constantly. Pour the cream mixture into the saucepan and cook, whisking constantly, until the mixture boils. Boil for 1 minute, whisking constantly. Remove from the heat.

Add the Parmesan.

Add salt and white pepper to taste.

CITRUS FRUIT GARNISH

(8 servings)

3 large oranges
3 small grapefruit
lettuce
8 maraschino cherries
POPPY SEED–HONEY DRESSING *(page 56)*

Peel and section the oranges and grapefruit.

Arrange lettuce leaves on each of 8 plates.

Alternate orange and grapefruit sections so that they form the shape of half of a fruit.

Top with a maraschino cherry.

Serve with Poppy Seed–Honey Dressing.

POPPY SEED–HONEY DRESSING

(1 cup)

¼ cup cider vinegar
¼ cup honey
½ teaspoon dry mustard
1 teaspoon celery salt
½ teaspoon poppy seeds
½ teaspoon onion juice
½ cup vegetable oil

Combine the vinegar, honey, and mustard in a saucepan. Bring to a boil, reduce the heat, and simmer, uncovered, for 2 minutes. Cool.

Add the celery salt, poppy seeds, and onion juice. Mix well.

Add the oil slowly, whisking constantly.

STRAWBERRY CAKE

½ cup unsalted butter
1 cup sugar
2 cups cake flour, sifted twice
½ teaspoon salt
2 teaspoons baking powder
⅔ cup milk
1 teaspoon vanilla
¼ teaspoon almond extract
4 egg whites
1 pint fresh strawberries or *1 box (10 ounces) frozen sliced strawberries*
1 cup whipping cream

Preheat the oven to 350° F.

Grease well and lightly flour the bottom and sides of 2 8-inch round cake pans. Line the bottom of each pan with a circle of waxed paper.

Cream the butter and sugar until light and fluffy.

Sift the cake flour, salt, and baking powder together.

Add the dry ingredients and milk alternately, beating constantly.

Add the vanilla and almond extracts.

Beat the egg whites until stiff peaks form. Fold them into the batter.

Pour into the prepared pans.

Bake at 350° F. for 30 to 35 minutes or until done. Do not overbake.

Cool in the pans for 10 minutes before turning out onto racks.

Slice the fresh strawberries or drain the frozen ones. Reserve a few for garnish.

Whip the cream until stiff.

Cover the bottom layer completely with a ¼-inch layer of whipped cream.

Cover the whipped cream with strawberries, leaving a margin of 1½ inches around the outer edge.

Cover the berries with a thin layer of whipped cream.

Place the second layer on top and frost the cake with whipped cream.

Garnish with the reserved strawberries.

Chill thoroughly.

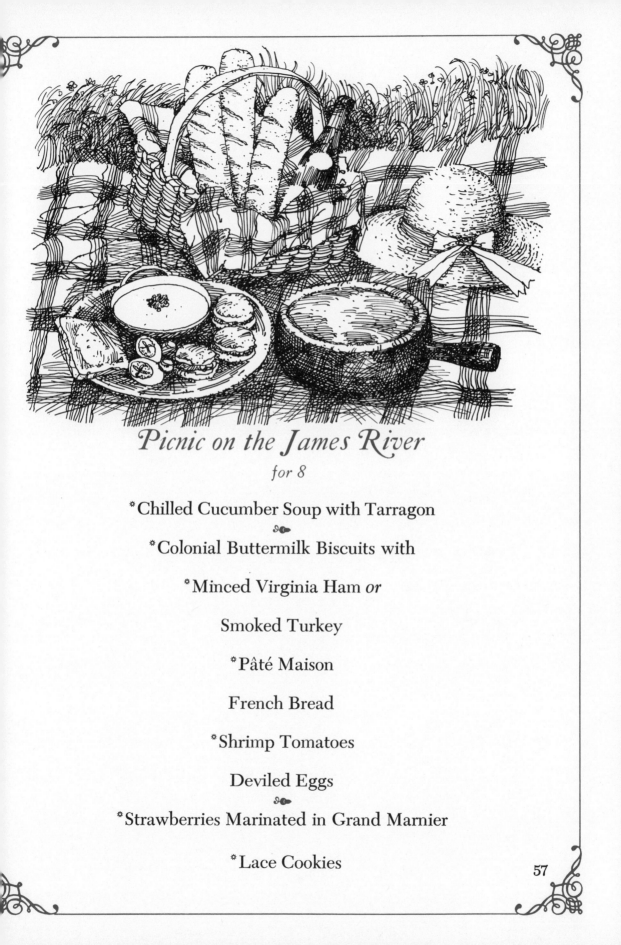

Picnic on the James River

for 8

*Chilled Cucumber Soup with Tarragon

*Colonial Buttermilk Biscuits with

*Minced Virginia Ham *or*

Smoked Turkey

*Pâté Maison

French Bread

*Shrimp Tomatoes

Deviled Eggs

*Strawberries Marinated in Grand Marnier

*Lace Cookies

CHILLED CUCUMBER SOUP WITH TARRAGON

(8 servings)

3 large cucumbers
¼ cup butter
¼ cup flour
3 cups CHICKEN STOCK *(page 30)* or *canned chicken broth*
2 cups milk
2 medium onions, chopped
1½ teaspoons tarragon
salt and white pepper
1 cup whipping cream
fresh tarragon leaves, chopped

Peel and halve the cucumbers. Scoop out the seeds and slice the cucumbers thinly. Reserve 8 slices for garnish.

Melt the butter in a saucepan. Add the cucumbers and simmer, covered, for 10 minutes. Stir in the flour and cook, uncovered, for 5 minutes.

Heat the Chicken Stock and add it to the mixture, whisking until the mixture is smooth and thick.

Combine the milk, onions, and tarragon and simmer over low heat for 10 minutes. Strain the milk into the cucumber mixture and bring to a simmer, whisking constantly. Simmer, covered, over very low heat for 15 minutes.

Purée the soup in a food processor or blender. Strain.

Add salt and white pepper to taste.

Chill thoroughly.

Taste for seasoning after the soup is chilled.

Stir in the cream just before serving.

Garnish with the reserved cucumber slices and chopped fresh tarragon leaves.

COLONIAL BUTTERMILK BISCUITS

(see page 13)

MINCED VIRGINIA HAM

(see page 50)

PÂTÉ MAISON

½ pound sliced bacon
water
1 tablespoon butter
1 onion, finely chopped
1 pound pork, fat and lean, ground
½ pound veal, ground
½ pound chicken livers, finely chopped
2 cloves garlic, pressed
⅛ teaspoon nutmeg
½ teaspoon thyme
⅛ teaspoon cloves
2 teaspoons salt
¾ teaspoon freshly ground pepper
3 tablespoons brandy
2 eggs
½ pound boiled ham, cut in 1 piece
2 small bay leaves

Preheat the oven to 350° F.

Cover the bacon with water. Bring to a boil, reduce the heat, and simmer, uncovered, for 10 minutes. Drain. Rinse with cold water. Reserve.

Melt the butter in a small skillet. Add the onion and sauté over medium heat until soft. Transfer to a mixing bowl.

Add the pork, veal, chicken livers, and garlic. Beat with an electric mixer for 3 minutes.

Combine the nutmeg, thyme, cloves, salt, pepper, brandy, and eggs in a small bowl. Beat until well blended. Add to the meat mixture. Mix well.

Slice the ham into strips ¼ inch wide.

Line a 1½-quart terrine with a cover with the bacon. Arrange the strips so that there will be enough overhang to cover the pâté after the terrine is filled.

Spread ⅓ of the pâté mixture in the bottom of the terrine. Lay ½ of the ham strips on top of the pâté mixture. Cover with ⅓ of the pâté mixture. Lay the rest of the strips on top. Cover with the final ⅓ of the pâté.

Fold the bacon over the top. Place the bay leaves on top of the bacon. Cover with a double thickness of aluminum foil. Put the lid on the terrine.

Place the terrine in a roasting pan. Fill the pan with enough hot water to come ⅔ of the way up the sides of the terrine.

Bake at 350° F. for 1½ hours.

Remove the terrine from the water bath. Take off the lid and put a bread board on top of the pâté. Weight it down with a heavy object.

Cool completely. Refrigerate, covered, for at least 2 days.

Note: The meats for the pâté should be very finely ground. Use a food processor or meat grinder.

SHRIMP TOMATOES

(2–3 dozen)

½ cup sour cream
2 ounces cream cheese
2 teaspoons shallot, minced
1½ teaspoons dill weed or
3 teaspoons fresh dill, minced
1 teaspoon parsley, chopped
⅛ teaspoon white pepper
1 basket cherry tomatoes
salt
6 ounces baby shrimp, cooked

Purée the sour cream, cream cheese, shallot, dill, parsley, and white pepper in a food processor or blender. Cover and let stand for 30 minutes.

Wash the tomatoes and dry them on paper towels.

Hollow out the stem ends. Sprinkle the centers of the tomatoes lightly with salt. Turn the tomatoes upside down on a rack to drain for 15 minutes.

Fill the centers with the mixture.

Top each tomato with 2 or 3 baby shrimp.

STRAWBERRIES MARINATED IN GRAND MARNIER

(8 servings)

William Byrd II noted the proliferation of wild strawberries in his *Natural History of Virginia*: "All the woods, fields and gardens are full of strawberries, which grow excellently well in this beautiful and lovely land."

Springtime still brings the succulent red berries, which are delicious used in the following recipe.

2 quarts ripe strawberries
1 cup light brown sugar
½ cup Grand Marnier

Wash the strawberries quickly and dry them on paper towels.

Hull the berries. Place them in a glass bowl.

Approximately 1 hour before serving, toss the strawberries gently with the brown sugar and Grand Marnier.

LACE COOKIES

(4–5 dozen)

½ cup vegetable shortening
⅓ cup sugar
⅓ cup brown sugar
1 egg
2 teaspoons vanilla
¼ cup all-purpose flour
½ teaspoon baking powder
⅛ teaspoon salt
1 cup rolled oats
⅓ cup pecans, ground

Preheat the oven to 325° F.

Line baking sheets with aluminum foil.

Cream the shortening and sugars until light and fluffy.

Add the egg and vanilla. Beat well.

Sift the flour, baking powder, and salt together. Add to the mixture. Mix well.

Add the rolled oats and pecans. Mix well.

Drop by half-teaspoonfuls onto the prepared baking sheets 3 inches apart.

Bake at 325° F. for 10 minutes.

Let the cookies cool slightly before peeling them from the foil.

Dinner

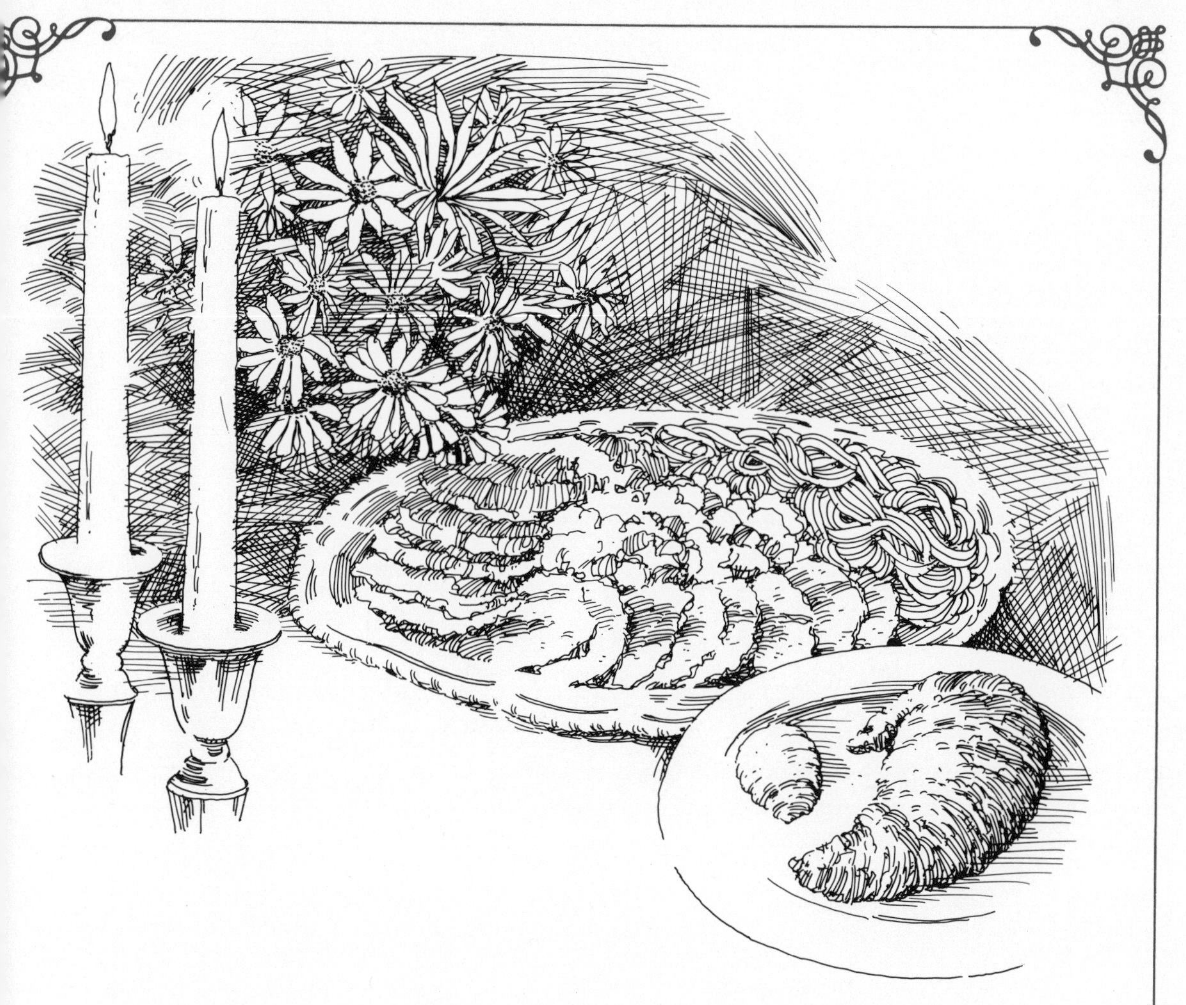

Dinner for Eight at the Williamsburg Inn

for 8

*Vichyssoise Supreme

*Veal Piccata, Sauté Bellevue

Green Noodles

*Salsify Sautéed with Fine Herbs

*Special Regency Salad

*Inn Dressing

*Snowballs

VICHYSSOISE SUPREME

(8 servings)

¼ cup unsalted butter
1 cup leeks, diced
½ cup onion, chopped
3 cups potatoes, thinly sliced
1 bay leaf
4 cups CHICKEN STOCK *(page 30)* or *canned chicken broth*
1 cup water
2 cups milk
salt and white pepper
2 cups whipping cream
2 tablespoons chives, chopped

Melt the butter in a heavy saucepan. Add the leeks and onion and sauté over medium heat until the vegetables are tender. Do not brown.

Add the potatoes, bay leaf, Chicken Stock, and water. Bring to a boil, reduce the heat, and simmer, uncovered, for 20 minutes or until the potatoes are soft.

Discard the bay leaf. Purée the soup in a food processor or blender.

Return to the heat and add the milk. Simmer for 10 minutes. Strain. Add salt and white pepper to taste.

Chill thoroughly.

Taste for seasoning after the soup is chilled.

Stir in the cream just before serving.

Garnish with the chopped chives.

VEAL PICCATA, SAUTÉ BELLEVUE

(8 servings)

1 ounce dried chanterelle mushrooms or *½ pound fresh mushrooms, thinly sliced*
2 pounds veal scaloppini
flour
unsalted butter
2 tablespoons shallot, chopped
2 tablespoons Madeira
1 cup CHICKEN STOCK *(page 30)* or *canned chicken broth*
2 teaspoons lemon juice
salt and pepper
2 ripe tomatoes, peeled and chopped
green noodles

Soak the chanterelle mushrooms in warm water while proceeding with the recipe. Drain and rinse well before using.

Pound the scaloppini between 2 pieces of waxed paper until flat. Dredge the scaloppini in flour.

Melt 2 tablespoons of butter in a heavy skillet. Sauté as many scaloppini as the skillet will hold over medium heat for 2 to 3 minutes on each side. As the scaloppini are cooked, arrange them on a heatproof platter. Add more butter as needed. Continue sautéing until all of the scaloppini are cooked. Keep warm.

Discard any butter remaining in the skillet. Melt 2 tablespoons of fresh butter. Add the shallot and sauté over medium heat until soft. Do not brown.

Add the Madeira and bring to a boil, stirring with a fork to deglaze the bottom of the skillet.

Add the Chicken Stock and mushrooms. Bring to a boil, reduce the heat, and simmer, covered, for 10 minutes.

Add the lemon juice and salt and pepper to taste.

Pour the sauce over the scaloppini.

Garnish with the chopped tomatoes.

Serve with green noodles.

John Randolph of Williamsburg wrote *A Treatise on Gardening* that contains seasonal advice on growing plants. Randolph noted that salsify is "A very excellent vegetable, but require[s] nicety in cooking . . . They are delicious in whatever way they can be dressed." Mrs. Raffald suggested that salsify could be boiled, stewed, or baked in scallop shells with bread crumbs, "or, make them into cakes, and fry them." Chefs at the Williamsburg Inn believe that the simplest way of fixing salsify is the best, as the following recipe attests.

SALSIFY SAUTÉED WITH FINE HERBS

(8 servings)

1 can (1 pound, 12 ounces) salsify
¼ cup butter
salt and white pepper
1 tablespoon parsley, chopped

Drain the salsify. Rinse with cold water. Dry on paper towels.

Melt the butter in a skillet. Add the salsify and toss over medium heat until heated through.

Add salt and white pepper to taste.

Sprinkle with the chopped parsley.

SPECIAL REGENCY SALAD

(8 servings)

1 head Boston lettuce
1 head romaine lettuce
1 bunch watercress
1 can (14 ounces) hearts of palm, drained
1 cup INN DRESSING *(page 64)*
16 pitted black olives, halved
16 cherry tomatoes

Tear the lettuce into small pieces.
Remove the stem ends from the watercress.
Slice the hearts of palm in ¼-inch slices.
Toss the lettuce, watercress, and hearts of palm with 1 cup of Inn Dressing.
Garnish with the halved black olives and cherry tomatoes.

INN DRESSING

(2 cups)

2 teaspoons flour
1 cup Chicken Stock *(page 30)* or *canned chicken broth*
2 teaspoons onion, minced
½ clove garlic
½ cup vegetable oil
1 tablespoon Dijon mustard
¼ cup white vinegar
1 egg yolk, lightly beaten
salt and white pepper
¼ cup olive oil

Combine the flour and Chicken Stock in a saucepan. Bring to a boil, reduce heat, and cook over medium heat for 5 minutes, stirring constantly. Remove from the heat.
Purée the onion, garlic, and vegetable oil in a food processor or blender. Strain the mixture into a mixing bowl.
Add the mustard, vinegar, and egg yolk.
Add salt and white pepper to taste.
Add the olive oil slowly, beating constantly with an electric mixer.
Beat in the Chicken Stock.

SNOWBALLS

(8 servings)

1 quart vanilla ice cream
2 cups coconut, shredded
1½ cups Chocolate Sauce *(page 80)*

Scoop the ice cream into 8 balls. Let them soften slightly.
Roll the ice cream balls in the shredded coconut. Place in the freezer and let harden before serving.
Place 3 tablespoons of Chocolate Sauce in each of 8 individual serving dishes. Place the snowballs on top of the Chocolate Sauce.

The Cascades Country Buffet

for 12

*Baked Virginia Ham

*Southern Fried Chicken

*Candied Sweet Potatoes

Black-eyed Peas

*Okra and Stewed Tomatoes

*Marinated Vegetables

*Corn Fritters with Honey

*Peach Cobbler *or*

*Southern Nut Pie

BAKED VIRGINIA HAM

Visitors to Williamsburg who plan to carry home a Virginia ham as a souvenir are advised to heed these preliminary directions or they may be sadly disappointed:

Scrub the ham to remove the coating of seasonings, cover it with water, and soak it for 24 hours.

Place the ham, skin side down, in a pan with enough fresh water to cover, bring to a boil, reduce the heat, and simmer, covered, for 20 to 25 minutes per pound.

When done, skin the ham and trim off excess fat.

Note: These directions apply to a Virginia ham that has been cured for at least 12 months. If the ham has been cured less than 12 months, follow the instructions on the wrapper or hang the ham and allow it to age.

1 10- to 12-pound Virginia ham
2 tablespoons light brown sugar
1 tablespoon bread crumbs
1 teaspoon cloves
3 teaspoons honey, dry sherry, or *sweet pickle vinegar*

Preheat the oven to 375° F.

Combine the brown sugar, bread crumbs, and cloves. Press the mixture into the ham.

Place the ham in a roasting pan. Bake at 375° F. for 15 minutes or until the sugar melts.

Drizzle honey, sherry, or sweet pickle vinegar over the ham. Bake at 375° F. for 15 minutes.

SOUTHERN FRIED CHICKEN

(12 servings)

2 broiler-fryers (3 to 3½ pounds each)
flour
4 eggs
2 tablespoons water
4 cups soft bread crumbs
1 teaspoon salt
⅛ teaspoon white pepper
⅛ teaspoon cayenne
vegetable oil

Line a baking sheet with waxed paper.

Cut each chicken into 8 pieces. Dredge with flour.

Beat the eggs and water together until well blended in a shallow bowl.

Combine the bread crumbs, salt, white pepper, and cayenne. Spread them on a large platter.

Dip each piece of chicken in the egg mixture, then lightly in the bread crumbs, then in the egg mixture, and finally coat well with bread crumbs. Place the pieces on the prepared baking sheet.

Refrigerate, covered with waxed paper, for 1 hour.

Heat 1¼ inches of oil to 375° F. in each of 2 large deep skillets. Fry the pieces of chicken for 3 minutes. Turn each piece over with kitchen tongs. Fry for 3 minutes and turn again. Continue frying and turning each piece every 5 minutes until the chicken is tender. Do not overcook.

Drain on paper towels.

CANDIED SWEET POTATOES

(12 servings)

3 cans (1 pound, 13 ounces each) sweet potatoes
¾ cup butter
1 cup light brown sugar
1½ teaspoons cinnamon
½ teaspoon nutmeg
¼ teaspoon cloves
2 teaspoons lemon rind, grated
1 tablespoon lemon juice
½ cup sherry
salt and pepper

Preheat the oven to 300° F.

Butter a 13 x 9 x 2-inch casserole.

Drain the sweet potatoes and slice them lengthwise. Place the sweet potatoes in the prepared casserole.

Combine the butter, brown sugar, cinnamon, nutmeg, cloves, lemon rind, lemon juice, and sherry in a saucepan. Heat until the butter melts and the sugar dissolves.

Add salt and pepper to taste.

Pour the mixture over the sweet potatoes.

Bake at 300° F. for 30 minutes.

OKRA AND STEWED TOMATOES

(12 servings)

2 tablespoons butter
2 tablespoons olive oil
1 cup onion, chopped
3 packages (10 ounces each) frozen okra, partially thawed
4 cups plum tomatoes, drained
½ teaspoon basil
salt and pepper

Heat the butter and oil in a saucepan. Add the onion and sauté over medium heat until soft.

Add the okra, tomatoes, basil, and salt and pepper to taste.

Simmer for 10 to 15 minutes or until the okra is tender.

MARINATED VEGETABLES

(12 servings)

1½ cups string beans
1 cauliflower
3 cups broccoli flowerets
2 cups carrot, diced
2 ripe tomatoes, diced
1 clove garlic, minced
½ cup vinegar
¾ cup olive oil
salt and pepper
1 tablespoon parsley, chopped

Cut the string beans, cauliflower, and broccoli flowerets into bite-size pieces.

Cook the string beans, cauliflower, broccoli, and carrot separately in boiling salted water until tender. Drain. Rinse with cold water. Dry on paper towels.

Place the cooked vegetables in a glass bowl.

Add the tomatoes, garlic, vinegar, and olive oil. Mix well.

Add salt and pepper to taste.

Chill thoroughly.

Sprinkle with the chopped parsley.

CORN FRITTERS WITH HONEY

(2 dozen)

1 egg
1½ cups milk
1½ tablespoons butter, melted
1½ cups all-purpose flour
½ cup cake flour
½ teaspoon baking powder
1 teaspoon salt
1½ teaspoons sugar
1 can (12 ounces) whole kernel corn, drained
vegetable oil
honey

Beat the egg until light.

Add the milk and melted butter.

Sift the flours, baking powder, salt, and sugar together. Add to the egg mixture.

Add the drained corn. Mix well.

Refrigerate the batter for at least 2 hours.

Drop by tablespoonfuls into deep hot fat (375° F.) and fry for 3 to 5 minutes. Do not fry more than 4 or 5 fritters at a time.

Drain on paper towels.

Serve with warm honey.

PEACH COBBLER

(12 servings)

6 cups fresh or *sliced canned peaches*
½ cup peach juice
4 eggs, divided
2 teaspoons lemon juice
1 cup sugar, divided
4 cups all-purpose flour
1 teaspoon salt
4 teaspoons baking powder
10 tablespoons butter
1¼ cups milk

Veal Piccata, Sauté Bellevue is the main course at an elegant Dinner for Eight at the Williamsburg Inn. ►

Preheat the oven to 425° F.

Butter a 13 x 9 x 2-inch casserole.

Peel and slice the fresh peaches ½ inch thick over a bowl to catch the juice or drain the canned peaches, reserving ½ cup of the syrup.

Beat 2 eggs well. Add the peach juice, lemon juice, and ½ cup of sugar. Mix well. Add the peach slices.

Spread the fruit mixture over the bottom of the prepared casserole.

Combine the flour, salt, baking powder, and ½ cup of sugar in a bowl. Cut in the butter with knives or a pastry blender until the mixture is mealy.

Beat 2 eggs and the milk together until well blended. Add to the flour mixture. Mix just long enough to moisten completely.

Spoon the dough over the peaches. Smooth it evenly with a spatula.

Bake at 425° F. for 30 minutes.

SOUTHERN NUT PIE

(2 pies)

2 9-inch unbaked Pie Shells *(page 40)*
6 eggs
1¼ cups light brown sugar
2¼ cups light corn syrup
2 teaspoons vanilla, divided
3 tablespoons butter, melted
1½ cups peanuts, finely ground
2 cups seedless raisins (optional)
1 cup whipping cream
¼ cup confectioners' sugar

Preheat the oven to 350° F. 10 minutes before the pies are ready to be baked.

Double the Pie Shell recipe. Do not bake the shells.

Beat the eggs well. Add the brown sugar, corn syrup, and 1½ teaspoons of vanilla. Mix well.

Add the melted butter and peanuts.

Add the raisins if desired.

Pour the mixture into the pie crust shells.

Bake at 350° F. for 40 minutes.

Cool on a rack.

Whip the cream until stiff. Add the confectioners' sugar and ½ teaspoon of vanilla.

Garnish the pies with the sweetened whipped cream.

◄ *The romantic ambience of a Late Supper in the Williamsburg Inn Regency Lounge is complemented by a menu that includes Virginia Crabmeat, Sauté Randolph and Broccoli Polonaise. Consommé Double with Dry Sack and Mocha Mousse begin and end the meal.*

Chesapeake Bay Feast Buffet

for 12

*Tidewater Crab Soup

Cold Table

Iced Clams on the Half Shell

*Scallops Seviche

*Marinated Eggplant and Tuna Salad

Hot Table

*Seafood Newburg

Steamed Rice

Buttered Peas

Dessert

*Peach and Pear Tarts

TIDEWATER CRAB SOUP

(12 servings)

2 pounds crabmeat
¼ cup unsalted butter
¼ cup shallot, minced
FISH STOCK *(below)*
3 cups whipping cream
½ cup Sauterne
salt and white pepper

Pick over the crabmeat. Discard any bits of shell or cartilage.

Melt the butter in a saucepan. Add the shallot and sauté over medium heat for 2 minutes. Do not brown.

Add the crabmeat and sauté for 3 minutes, stirring constantly.

Add the Fish Stock and cream. Bring to a simmer.

Add the Sauterne and salt and white pepper to taste. Simmer, uncovered, over very low heat for 15 to 20 minutes.

FISH STOCK

(7 cups)

3 pounds fish bones, heads, and tails
7 cups water
1 bay leaf
½ teaspoon thyme

Cover the fish trimmings with the water.

Add the bay leaf and thyme.

Bring to a boil, reduce the heat, and simmer, uncovered, for 20 minutes.

Strain the stock.

SCALLOPS SEVICHE

(12 servings)

6 tablespoons lime juice
6 tablespoons lemon juice
3 pounds bay scallops
¼ cup onion, chopped
3 tablespoons parsley, chopped
6 tablespoons catsup
Tabasco sauce
salt and freshly ground pepper
sprigs of parsley

Combine the lime juice, lemon juice, and scallops. Mix well.

Refrigerate overnight.

Drain the scallops. Add the onion, parsley, catsup, 6 to 8 drops of Tabasco sauce, and salt and pepper to taste. Mix well.

Chill thoroughly.

Garnish with sprigs of parsley.

MARINATED EGGPLANT AND TUNA SALAD

(12 servings)

3 pounds eggplant
½ cup olive oil
1½ cups Creole Sauce *(page 24)*
1 can (12½ ounces) tuna, drained
2 tablespoons white vinegar
2 tablespoons lemon juice
1 teaspoon salt
¼ teaspoon oregano
¼ teaspoon thyme
¼ teaspoon basil
¼ teaspoon garlic powder
⅛ teaspoon white pepper

Peel the eggplant and cut into ½-inch dice.

Heat ¼ cup of oil in each of 2 large skillets. Add the eggplant and sauté over medium heat, stirring frequently, until the eggplant is tender but firm. Remove from the heat.

Add the Creole Sauce, tuna, vinegar, lemon juice, salt, oregano, thyme, basil, garlic powder, and white pepper. Mix well.

Refrigerate overnight.

SEAFOOD NEWBURG

(12 servings)

1 pound bay scallops
Court Bouillon *(page 73)*
1½ pounds medium shrimp, raw
10 tablespoons butter, divided
1 tablespoon Hungarian paprika
½ cup Amontillado sherry
½ cup flour
1 cup milk
4 egg yolks
1 cup whipping cream
11 ounces lobster meat, diced
salt and white pepper
steamed rice

Simmer the scallops in the Court Bouillon for 3 minutes. Drain. Reserve.

Bring the Court Bouillon to a boil. Add the shrimp and cook just until done. Drain, reserving the Court Bouillon. When the shrimp are cool enough to handle, peel and devein them.

Boil the Court Bouillon down until it measures 2 cups. Strain. Reserve.

Melt 2 tablespoons of butter in a small saucepan. Add the paprika and let stand over very low heat for 5 minutes. Remove from the heat. Add the sherry.

Melt 8 tablespoons of butter in a saucepan. Stir in the flour and cook over medium heat for 3 minutes, stirring constantly. Do not let the mixture brown.

Heat the milk and reserved 2 cups of Court Bouillon and add to the butter and flour mixture, whisking until the mixture is smooth and thick.

Beat the egg yolks and cream together until well blended. Add a little of the hot sauce, stirring constantly. Pour the cream mixture into the saucepan and cook, whisking constantly, until the mixture is almost to the boiling point. Reduce the heat.

Add the scallops, shrimp, and lobster meat and simmer until heated through.

Add salt and white pepper to taste.

Add the paprika mixture.

Serve over steamed rice.

Note: If small bay scallops are not available, sea scallops sliced in bite-size pieces may be substituted.

COURT BOUILLON

(5 cups)

4 cups water
1 cup white wine
1 small onion, sliced
1 small carrot, sliced
2 sprigs parsley
½ bay leaf
pinch of thyme
½ teaspoon salt

Combine the water, wine, onion, carrot, parsley, bay leaf, thyme, and salt in a saucepan. Bring to a boil, reduce the heat, and simmer, covered, for 10 minutes.

Strain the court bouillon through a double thickness of cheesecloth.

PEACH AND PEAR TARTS

(12 tarts)

PECAN PASTRY *(page 74)*
VANILLA CREAM CUSTARD *(page 74)*
6 fresh or *canned peach halves*
6 fresh or *canned pear halves*
2 tablespoons apricot jam, forced through a sieve
1 teaspoon sugar
1 teaspoon kirsch

Preheat the oven to 400° F. 10 minutes before the tarts are ready to be baked.

Lightly oil 12 3½-inch tart tins.

For easy handling, work with only ¼ of the Pecan Pastry at a time. Keep the rest refrigerated until ready to roll out.

Line the prepared tart tins with the pastry. Prick the bottoms and sides with a fork. Place waxed paper over the dough and fill the tins with dried beans to prevent the dough from rising.

Chill in the freezer for 20 minutes.

Bake at 400° F. for 10 minutes.

Remove from the oven, empty the beans, remove the waxed paper, prick the bottoms, and return to the oven for 5 minutes.

Cool completely.

Line the bottoms of the cooled tart shells with Vanilla Cream Custard.

Place a piece of fruit, cut side down, in each shell.

Combine the apricot jam and sugar in a small saucepan. Bring to a boil, stirring constantly. Remove from the heat.

Cool slightly before adding the kirsch.

Brush each piece of fruit twice with the glaze.

PECAN PASTRY

(12 tart shells)

¾ cup pecans, finely ground
1 cup all-purpose flour
1 tablespoon sugar
¼ teaspoon salt
½ cup unsalted butter
¼ cup ice water

Place the pecans, flour, sugar, salt, and butter, cut into small pieces, in the bowl of a food processor. Process briefly until the mixture is mealy.

Add the ice water. Process for 50 seconds or until the mixture forms a ball.

Wrap the dough in waxed paper. Refrigerate for 1 hour.

VANILLA CREAM CUSTARD

(3 cups)

½ cup sugar
2 tablespoons cornstarch
5 egg yolks
2 cups milk
1 teaspoon vanilla

Combine the sugar and cornstarch. Add the egg yolks. Beat well.

Scald the milk. Gradually pour it over the egg mixture, beating constantly.

Bring almost to a boil and cook, stirring constantly, for 2 minutes. Remove from the heat.

Cool slightly before adding the vanilla.

Chill thoroughly.

Cascades Specialties

for 8

*Deviled Cherrystone Clams

*Glazed Roast Loin of Pork with

*Apple Brandy Sauce

*Baked Apple Garnish

*Rissolé Potatoes

*Spinach Casserole

*Special Cascades Ice Cream Dessert

*Chocolate Sauce

DEVILED CHERRYSTONE CLAMS

(8 servings)

4 slices lean bacon
¼ cup butter
¼ cup green onion, minced
¼ cup green pepper, minced
¼ cup celery, minced
2 tablespoons parsley, minced
1 teaspoon dry mustard
½ teaspoon Worcestershire sauce
1 teaspoon lemon juice
1 tablespoon pimiento, minced
16 cherrystone clams, cooked and chopped
Tabasco sauce
salt and pepper
¼ cup bread crumbs

Preheat the oven to 425° F.

Lightly butter 16 clean clam shells. Place them securely on a bed of rock salt in a large pan or in 8 individual serving dishes.

Fry the bacon until it is very crisp. Drain well. Crumble the bacon. Reserve.

Melt the butter in a skillet. Add the green onion, green pepper, celery, and parsley and sauté over medium heat until the vegetables are tender. Do not brown. Remove from the heat.

Add the mustard, Worcestershire sauce, lemon juice, pimiento, clams, and 4 drops of Tabasco sauce.

Season to taste with salt and pepper.

Stuff the prepared clam shells with the clam mixture. Top with the bread crumbs and crumbled bacon.

Bake at 425° F. for 10 minutes. Brown quickly under the broiler.

Note: If fresh clams are not available, 1 cup of canned minced clams, well drained, may be substituted.

GLAZED ROAST LOIN OF PORK

1 7-pound center cut loin of pork roast
½ teaspoon powdered rosemary
1 teaspoon salt
¼ teaspoon pepper
Apple Brandy Glaze *(page 77)*
Apple Brandy Sauce *(page 77)*
Baked Apple Garnish *(page 77)*

Ask the butcher to separate the chine bone from the meat without cutting it off entirely.

Rub the pork with the rosemary, salt, and pepper and bring to room temperature.

Preheat the oven to 350° F.

Place the pork on a rack in a roasting pan and roast at 350° F.

for approximately 2½ to 3 hours or until the internal temperature reaches 185° F.

30 minutes before the end of the roasting time, remove all of the fat from the roasting pan, leaving the drippings. Brush the pork several times with the Apple Brandy Glaze. When it tests done, transfer the pork to a platter. Keep warm.

Remove all of the fat from the roasting pan, leaving the drippings.

Add the Apple Brandy Sauce and bring to a boil, stirring with a fork to deglaze the bottom of the pan. Taste for seasoning.

Strain into a warmed sauceboat.

Garnish the platter with the Baked Apples.

APPLE BRANDY GLAZE

(1¼ cups)

1 cup dark brown sugar
1 tablespoon dry mustard
1 teaspoon salt
¼ teaspoon pepper
⅛ teaspoon cloves
⅛ teaspoon allspice
¼ cup apple brandy

Combine the brown sugar, mustard, salt, pepper, cloves, allspice, and apple brandy. Mix well.

APPLE BRANDY SAUCE

(1½ cups)

¾ cup apple jelly
1 teaspoon lemon rind, grated
2 tablespoons lemon juice
1 teaspoon onion, grated
⅛ teaspoon ginger
1 teaspoon prepared horseradish
½ cup apple brandy

Combine the apple jelly, lemon rind, lemon juice, onion, ginger, prepared horseradish, and apple brandy. Mix well.

BAKED APPLE GARNISH

(8 servings)

4 baking apples
8 teaspoons apple jelly
2 tablespoons butter, melted
cinnamon
sugar

Preheat the oven to 350° F.

Butter an ovenproof casserole.

Cut the apples in half horizontally. Core them. Place the apple halves in the prepared casserole.

Place 1 teaspoon of apple jelly in the center of each apple. Brush the apple halves with melted butter, dust with a little cinnamon, and sprinkle with a little sugar.

Cover the casserole loosely with aluminum foil.

Bake at 350° F. for 20 minutes.

RISSOLÉ POTATOES

(8 servings)

Rissolé potatoes are a deliciously uncomplicated accompaniment to roast meats. Mrs. Bradley included several recipes featuring potatoes in her two-volume manual, *The British Housewife*, warning her readers to exercise care in preparing them because, although it "seems very easy, [it] is very often ill done; for one Plate of Potatoes that come to a Table as they should, ten are spoiled."

6 cups potato balls
2 tablespoons butter
2 tablespoons vegetable oil
salt and white pepper

Cut balls from large potatoes with a melon ball cutter. Place the balls in a pan of cold salted water.

Bring to a boil, reduce the heat, and simmer, uncovered, for 5 minutes. Drain. Dry the balls on paper towels.

Heat the butter and oil in a large skillet. Add the potato balls and sauté over medium heat for 15 minutes, tossing frequently so that they brown evenly.

Add salt and white pepper to taste.

SPINACH CASSEROLE

(8 servings)

3 boxes (10 ounces each) frozen spinach
1½ cups water
1 teaspoon salt
2 tablespoons butter
1 package (8 ounces) cream cheese, cut in pieces
1 cup sour cream
¼ teaspoon nutmeg
salt and pepper

Preheat the oven to 300° F.

Butter a 1½-quart casserole.

Place the spinach in a heavy saucepan. Add the water and 1 teaspoon of salt. Bring to a boil and cook, covered, over high heat until thawed. Break up the spinach with a fork as soon as possible. Drain the spinach in a colander. Press out the excess moisture with the back of a wooden spoon.

Purée the spinach in a food processor or blender.

Add the butter, cream cheese, sour cream, and nutmeg and purée.

Add salt and pepper to taste.

Place the spinach in the prepared casserole.

Bake at 300° F. for 30 minutes.

SPECIAL CASCADES ICE CREAM DESSERT

(8 servings)

This recipe has been adapted from the delicious Cascades ice cream pie.

Spongecake *(below)*
1 quart peppermint ice cream
1 quart chocolate ice cream
6 egg whites
pinch of cream of tartar
⅔ cup super fine sugar
½ teaspoon vanilla
Chocolate Sauce *(page 80)*

Preheat the oven to 475° F. 10 minutes before the meringue is ready to be browned.

Place the Spongecake on an ovenproof plate or platter.

Spread the peppermint ice cream on top of the Spongecake. Freeze for 30 minutes.

Spread the chocolate ice cream on top of the peppermint ice cream. Freeze for 1 hour.

Beat the egg whites until frothy. Add a pinch of cream of tartar and beat until soft peaks form. Gradually add the sugar and beat until stiff peaks form.

Add the vanilla.

Fill a pastry bag fitted with a decorative tip with meringue.

Spread the rest of the meringue over the cake in a layer ¾ inch thick right down to the platter. Pipe meringue around the base of the dessert and make swirls on the top.

Freeze for 2 hours.

Bake at 475° F. for 3 minutes or until the meringue is lightly browned.

Serve with Chocolate Sauce.

SPONGECAKE

3 eggs, separated
½ cup sugar
1 teaspoon vanilla
pinch of cream of tartar
⅔ cup cake flour, measured after sifting
¼ cup butter, melted

Preheat the oven to 350° F.

Grease well and lightly flour the bottom and sides of a 9-inch round cake pan.

Beat the egg yolks with an electric mixer for 1 minute. Gradually add the sugar and beat for 4 minutes. Add the vanilla.

Beat the egg whites until foamy. Add the pinch of cream of tartar and beat until stiff peaks form.

Lightly and delicately fold ¼ of the whites into the yolks mixture. Then fold in ⅓ of the flour, ¼ of the whites, ⅓ of the flour, ¼ of the whites, ⅓ of the flour, and the remaining ¼ of the whites.

Add the butter, folding just enough to mix well. Pour into the prepared pan.

Bake at 350° F. for 20 minutes or until done. Do not overbake.

Cool in the pan for 10 minutes before turning out onto a rack.

CHOCOLATE SAUCE

(3 cups)

4 ounces unsweetened chocolate
2 tablespoons butter
½ cup hot coffee
½ cup boiling water
2 cups sugar
¼ cup light corn syrup
½ cup whipping cream
2 tablespoons sweet sherry

Melt the chocolate in the top of a double boiler over hot water.

Combine the butter, coffee, boiling water, sugar, corn syrup, and cream. Mix well.

Add the melted chocolate.

Cook over medium heat, stirring constantly, until the mixture begins to boil. Reduce the heat and boil gently, without stirring, for 7 minutes. Remove from the heat.

Add the sherry.

Dinner at King's Arms Tavern

for 4

*Mobjack Bay Oysters on the Half Shell

*Spicy Cocktail Sauce

*Cornish Game Hens in Casserole
with Garden Vegetables

*White Burgundy Wine Sauce

*Watercress and Artichoke Hearts Salad

*Lemon–Olive Oil Dressing

*Rum Raisin Ice Cream

MOBJACK BAY OYSTERS ON THE HALF SHELL

(4 servings)

Colonial Virginians did not agree with Jonathan Swift's observation that "he was a bold man that first eat an oyster"; oysters "laid on their Shells in a Dish" were as popular in the eighteenth century as they are today. Mrs. Bradley's advice still pertains too: "The Perfection of the Oyster is in its being alive, healthy, and properly relished . . . Oisters should always be eaten in the Shell the Moment they are opened."

24 oysters
SPICY COCKTAIL SAUCE *(page 12)*

Open the oysters and lay them in their shells on a bed of crushed ice.

Serve with Spicy Cocktail Sauce.

SPICY COCKTAIL SAUCE

(see page 12)

CORNISH GAME HENS IN CASSEROLE WITH GARDEN VEGETABLES

(4 servings)

¼ cup butter, divided
4 Cornish game hens
salt and pepper
½ pound button mushrooms
16 pearl onions
1 carrot, coarsely diced
¾ cup peas
¾ cup string beans
¼ cup white Burgundy wine
WHITE BURGUNDY WINE SAUCE *(page 83)*

Preheat the oven to 450° F.

Butter 4 individual casseroles.

Melt 3 tablespoons of butter.

Place the Cornish game hens, breast up, on a rack in a roasting pan. Brush with the melted butter and sprinkle with salt and pepper.

Reduce the heat to 350° F. and roast the game hens until they test done, about 1 hour. Baste occasionally with the pan drippings.

Melt 1 tablespoon of butter in a skillet. Add the mushrooms and sauté over medium heat for 2 to 3 minutes. Reserve.

Cook the pearl onions, carrot, peas, and string beans separately in boiling salted water until tender. Drain. Reserve.

When the game hens are roasted, transfer them to the prepared casseroles.

Remove all of the fat from the roasting pan, leaving the drippings.

Add the wine and bring to a boil, stirring with a fork to deglaze the bottom of the pan. Strain into the White Burgundy Wine Sauce. Taste for seasoning.

Preheat the oven to 400° F.

Pour the White Burgundy Wine Sauce over the game hens. Sprinkle with the reserved vegetables.

Bake at 400° F. for 10 minutes or until heated through.

WHITE BURGUNDY WINE SAUCE

(3 cups)

¼ cup butter
¼ cup flour
2 cups Chicken Stock *(page 30)* or *canned chicken broth*
salt and white pepper
½ cup white Burgundy wine

Melt the butter in a saucepan. Stir in the flour and cook over medium heat for 3 minutes, stirring constantly. Do not let the mixture brown.

Heat the Chicken Stock and add it to the mixture, whisking until the mixture is smooth and thick.

Add salt and white pepper to taste.

Add the white Burgundy wine and simmer, uncovered, for 10 minutes.

WATERCRESS AND ARTICHOKE HEARTS SALAD

(4 servings)

1 can (14 ounces) artichoke hearts or *1 package (9 ounces) frozen artichoke hearts*
1 bunch watercress
½ cup Lemon–Olive Oil Dressing *(page 84)*

Drain the canned artichoke hearts, rinse with cold water, and dry on paper towels or cook the frozen artichoke hearts, drain, and cool.

Cut the artichoke hearts in half.

Remove the stem ends from the watercress.

Pour the Lemon–Olive Oil Dressing over the artichoke hearts. Toss gently.

Chill thoroughly.

Just before serving, toss the artichoke hearts with the watercress.

LEMON–OLIVE OIL DRESSING

(1 cup)

¼ cup lemon juice
1 teaspoon salt
¼ teaspoon white pepper
1 teaspoon sugar
1 teaspoon lemon rind, grated
Tabasco sauce
¾ cup olive oil

Combine the lemon juice, salt, white pepper, sugar, grated lemon rind, and 4 to 6 drops of Tabasco sauce. Mix well.

Add the olive oil slowly, whisking constantly.

RUM RAISIN ICE CREAM

(1½ quarts)

1 tablespoon cornstarch
4 cups milk, divided
2 egg yolks
¾ cup sugar
1 cup whipping cream
pinch of salt
yellow food coloring
½ teaspoon vanilla
2 tablespoons imitation rum extract
¾ cup dark seedless raisins

Dissolve the cornstarch in 1 cup of milk.

Beat the egg yolks well. Gradually add the sugar.

Combine 3 cups of milk and the cream. Add the cornstarch mixture and heat to the boiling point.

Gradually pour the hot milk and cream over the egg mixture, beating constantly.

Add the salt and a few drops of food coloring to give the mixture the color of rich cream.

Cook over medium heat, stirring constantly, until the mixture coats a spoon.

Pour the mixture into the freezer container of an electric ice cream maker.

Chill thoroughly.

Add the vanilla and rum extracts.

Follow the manufacturer's directions for freezing.

After 20 minutes of churning, add the raisins and finish freezing.

Chilled Cream of Watercress Soup and Roast Leg of Lamb highlight a joyous Mother's Day Celebration at the Williamsburg Inn. ►

Overleaf:
A wreath of finely chopped parsley garnishes a cup of Christmas Broth, the first course of a simple yet festively elegant Yuletide Supper.

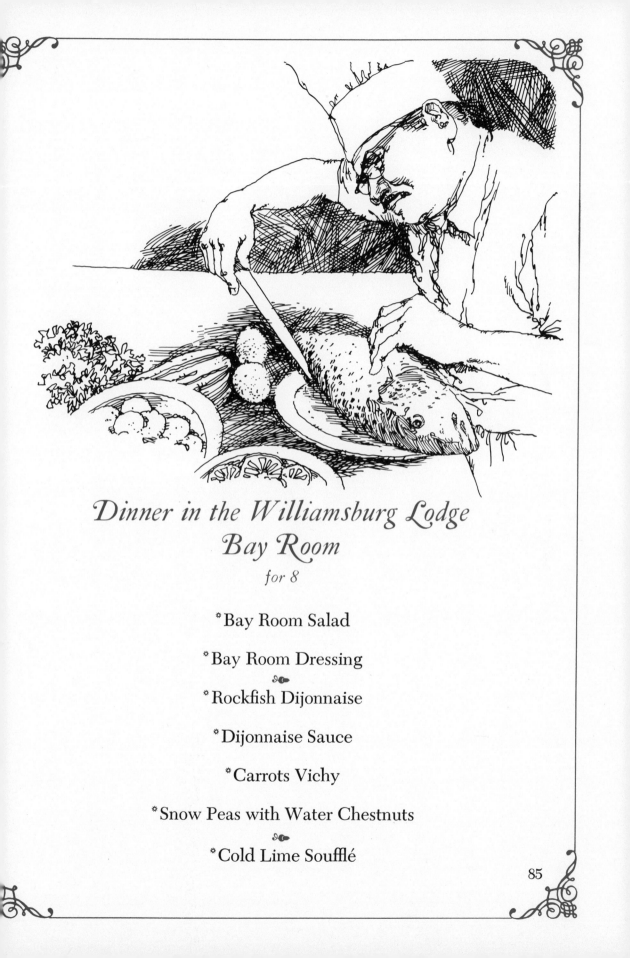

Dinner in the Williamsburg Lodge Bay Room

for 8

*Bay Room Salad

*Bay Room Dressing

*Rockfish Dijonnaise

*Dijonnaise Sauce

*Carrots Vichy

*Snow Peas with Water Chestnuts

*Cold Lime Soufflé

BAY ROOM SALAD

(8 servings)

4 cups water
1 thick slice onion
1 teaspoon salt
1 tablespoon white vinegar
½ pound bay scallops
¼ pound mushrooms, thinly sliced
1 teaspoon lemon juice
lettuce
1 pound baby shrimp, cooked
cherry tomatoes
2 tablespoons parsley, chopped
BAY ROOM DRESSING *(below)*

Combine the water, onion, salt, and vinegar in a saucepan. Bring to a boil, reduce the heat, and simmer, covered, for 5 minutes.

Add the scallops and simmer for 3 minutes. Drain. Cool.

Toss the mushrooms gently with the lemon juice.

Arrange lettuce leaves on each of 8 salad plates.

Arrange some scallops, mushrooms, and baby shrimp on each plate. Garnish with cherry tomatoes and chopped parsley.

Serve with Bay Room Dressing.

Note: If small bay scallops are not available, sea scallops sliced in bite-size pieces may be substituted.

BAY ROOM DRESSING

(1½ cups)

½ cup MAYONNAISE *(page 43)*
½ cup sour cream
½ cup buttermilk
2 anchovy fillets, minced
1½ teaspoons dehydrated onion
⅛ teaspoon onion powder
1 teaspoon lemon juice
⅛ teaspoon celery salt

Combine the Mayonnaise, sour cream, buttermilk, anchovy fillets, dehydrated onion, onion powder, lemon juice, and celery salt. Mix well.

Refrigerate overnight.

ROCKFISH DIJONNAISE

(8 servings)

2 cups water
½ onion, sliced
½ carrot, sliced
2 teaspoons salt
¼ teaspoon white pepper
1 cup dry white wine
1 bay leaf
¼ teaspoon thyme
8 fish fillets (6 ounces each)
DIJONNAISE SAUCE *(below)*

Preheat the oven to 350° F. 10 minutes before the fish is ready to be baked.

Combine the water, onion, carrot, salt, white pepper, wine, bay leaf, and thyme in a roasting pan. Bring to a boil, reduce the heat, and simmer, covered, for 15 minutes.

Add the fish fillets in 1 layer. Simmer for 6 minutes or just until cooked. Do not let the water boil.

Carefully remove the fillets to a baking sheet lined with a cloth towel. Cool.

Place the fillets on a heatproof platter. Spread each one with Dijonnaise Sauce.

Bake at 350° F. for 10 minutes. Brown quickly under the broiler.

Note: Striped bass, cod, haddock, or flounder may be substituted for the rockfish.

DIJONNAISE SAUCE

(¾ cup)

1 teaspoon butter
1 teaspoon flour
2 tablespoons milk
3 egg yolks
1 tablespoon lemon juice
3 tablespoons whipping cream
6 tablespoons butter, cut in small pieces
salt
cayenne
1½ teaspoons Dijon mustard

Melt 1 teaspoon of butter in a small saucepan. Stir in the flour and cook over medium heat for 3 minutes, stirring constantly. Do not let the mixture brown.

Add the milk, whisking until the cream sauce is thick and smooth. Reserve.

Whisk the egg yolks, lemon juice, and whipping cream over medium heat just until the mixture begins to thicken.

Remove from the heat and gradually add the 6 tablespoons of butter, whisking constantly.

Add salt and cayenne to taste.
Stir in the mustard and the reserved cream sauce.

CARROTS VICHY

(8 servings)

4 cups carrots, peeled and sliced ⅛ inch thick
Vichy or soda water
½ teaspoon salt
¼ cup butter
2 tablespoons sugar
salt and white pepper
1 tablespoon parsley, chopped

Place the carrots in a saucepan and cover with Vichy or soda water. Add the salt.

Cook, covered, until tender. Drain.

Melt the butter in a saucepan. Add the carrots and toss over medium heat until heated through.

Add the sugar.

Add salt and white pepper to taste.

Sprinkle with the chopped parsley.

SNOW PEAS WITH WATER CHESTNUTS

(8 servings)

¼ cup butter
3 packages (10 ounces each) frozen snow peas, thawed
1 can (8½ ounces) water chestnuts, drained and sliced
½ teaspoon sugar
2 teaspoons soy sauce

Melt the butter in a skillet. Add the snow peas and water chestnuts and toss over medium heat until heated through.

Add the sugar and soy sauce.

COLD LIME SOUFFLÉ

(8 servings)

1 tablespoon unflavored gelatin
½ cup cold water
5 egg yolks
1 cup sugar
2 cups milk
¾ cup fresh lime juice
rind of 1½ limes, grated
green food coloring
2 cups whipping cream, divided
2 teaspoons confectioners' sugar
8 lime slices

Dissolve the gelatin in the cold water.

Beat the egg yolks slightly.

Combine the sugar and milk. Stir until the sugar dissolves. Heat to the boiling point.

Gradually pour the hot milk mixture over the egg yolks, beating constantly.

Add the gelatin, lime juice, lime rind, and a few drops of food coloring. Mix well. Strain into a bowl.

Refrigerate, stirring occasionally, until the mixture begins to thicken and starts to set.

Whip 1½ cups of cream until stiff. Fold it into the soufflé mixture.

Pour into dessert glasses.

Refrigerate overnight.

Whip ½ cup of cream until stiff. Add the confectioners' sugar.

Garnish with the whipped cream and lime slices.

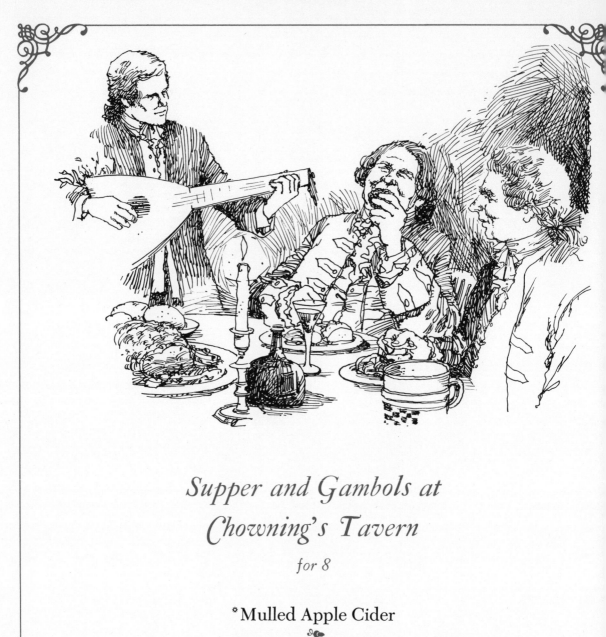

Supper and Gambols at Chowning's Tavern

for 8

*Mulled Apple Cider

*Barbecued Beef Ribs

*Barbecue Sauce

Tossed Salad

*Chutney Dressing

*Pecan Tarts

Josiah Chowning's reconstructed tavern is operated much like an eighteenth-century alehouse. "Gambols"—colonial games, music, entertainment, and various "diversions"—take place nightly at Josiah Chowning's Tavern.

MULLED APPLE CIDER

(8 mugs)

8 cups fresh apple cider
1 cup light brown sugar, lightly packed
½ cup lemon juice
½ teaspoon nutmeg
1 4-inch stick of cinnamon
8 whole cloves

Combine the cider, brown sugar, lemon juice, and nutmeg in a stainless steel or enamel saucepan.

Tie the cinnamon stick and cloves in a cheesecloth bag and place it in the pan.

Simmer for 10 minutes. Remove the bag of spices.

Serve hot.

BARBECUED BEEF RIBS

(8 servings)

8 pounds beef short ribs
⅔ cup cider vinegar
1 teaspoon salt
½ teaspoon freshly ground pepper
1 teaspoon curry powder
1½ teaspoons dry mustard
BARBECUE SAUCE *(page 92)*

Preheat the oven to 375° F.

Place the short ribs on racks in 2 roasting pans.

Sprinkle with the vinegar.

Combine the salt, pepper, curry powder, and mustard. Sprinkle the mixture over the short ribs.

Bake at 375° F. for 1 hour.

Cover with hot Barbecue Sauce.

BARBECUE SAUCE

(3 cups)

¾ cup catsup
½ cup red wine vinegar
1 cup water
½ cup vegetable oil
2 teaspoons dry mustard
2 tablespoons Worcestershire sauce
1 teaspoon salt
1 teaspoon paprika
⅛ teaspoon Tabasco sauce
2 slices lemon, seeded
1 medium onion, chopped
¼ cup honey

Combine the catsup, vinegar, water, oil, mustard, Worcestershire sauce, salt, paprika, Tabasco sauce, lemon slices, and onion in a saucepan. Bring to a boil, reduce the heat, and simmer, uncovered, for 20 minutes.

Strain through a fine sieve.

Add the honey. Mix well.

Serve hot.

CHUTNEY DRESSING

(1½ cups)

½ cup cider vinegar
¼ teaspoon dry mustard
½ teaspoon salt
⅛ teaspoon sugar
¼ teaspoon white pepper
¼ cup chutney, minced
¾ cup vegetable oil

Combine the vinegar and mustard. Mix well.

Add the salt, sugar, white pepper, and chutney. Mix well.

Add the oil slowly, whisking constantly.

PECAN TARTS

(8 tarts)

Thomas Jefferson thanked a friend who had sent him a box of "paccan nuts" from New Orleans, noting that "the Tree grows to the usual size of Forest Trees and affords a delightful shade in summer . . . the nuts I have immediately forwarded to Monticello, my residence in Virginia to be planted."

TART PASTRY *(below)*
4 eggs
¼ cup sugar
½ cup light brown sugar
½ teaspoon salt
1½ cups light corn syrup
1 tablespoon butter, melted
1½ teaspoons vanilla, divided
1 cup pecan halves
½ cup whipping cream
2 tablespoons confectioners' sugar
8 pecan halves

Preheat the oven to 400° F. 10 minutes before the tarts are ready to be baked.

Lightly oil 8 3½-inch tart pans.

Roll out the dough ⅛ inch thick on a lightly floured board or pastry cloth. Line the prepared tart pans with the pastry.

Place the tart shells in the freezer while making the filling.

Beat the eggs lightly. Add the sugars, salt, corn syrup, melted butter, and 1 teaspoon of vanilla. Mix well.

Divide the pecan halves among the tart shells. Pour the filling over them.

Place the tarts on a baking sheet.

Reduce the heat to 350° F.

Bake at 350° F. for 50 minutes.

Cool on a rack.

Whip the cream until stiff. Add the confectioners' sugar and ½ teaspoon of vanilla.

Garnish each tart with whipped cream and a pecan half.

TART PASTRY

(8 tart shells)

1½ cups all-purpose flour
½ teaspoon salt
2 teaspoons sugar
¼ cup vegetable shortening
¼ cup butter
¼ cup ice water
1½ teaspoons cider vinegar or *lemon juice*
1 egg yolk

Combine the flour, salt, and sugar. Mix well.

Cut in the shortening and butter with knives or a pastry blender until the mixture is mealy.

Beat the ice water, vinegar, and egg yolk together until well blended. Stir into the flour mixture. Mix well.

Wrap the dough in waxed paper. Refrigerate for 30 minutes.

Late Supper in the Williamsburg Inn Regency Lounge

for 4

*Consommé Double with Dry Sack

*Virginia Crabmeat, Sauté Randolph

*Broccoli Polonaise

*Mocha Mousse

CONSOMMÉ DOUBLE WITH DRY SACK

(4 servings)

8 cups Clear Consommé *(below)*
1 tablespoon lemon juice
¼ cup Dry Sack sherry
4 slices lemon
1 teaspoon parsley, minced

Boil the Clear Consommé over medium heat until it is reduced to 4 cups.

Just before serving, heat almost to the boiling point. Add the lemon juice and sherry.

Garnish each serving with a slice of lemon and a little parsley.

CLEAR CONSOMME

(2 quarts)

10 ounces ground beef
1 medium onion, finely chopped
2 cups celery, chopped
½ cup carrot, chopped
3 egg whites with shells
5 sprigs parsley
½ teaspoon thyme
2 cloves
1 bay leaf
6 peppercorns
1 cup plum tomatoes, drained and chopped
6 cups Beef Stock *(page 35)*
½ teaspoon salt

Combine the ground beef, onion, celery, carrot, egg whites and shells, parsley, thyme, cloves, bay leaf, peppercorns, tomatoes, Beef Stock, and salt in a soup pot. Bring to a boil, reduce the heat, and simmer, uncovered, for 1½ hours, removing any scum that appears on the surface.

Strain the stock and remove all fat.

Taste for seasoning.

VIRGINIA CRABMEAT, SAUTÉ RANDOLPH

(4 servings)

4 frozen patty shells
½ pound backfin crabmeat
2 teaspoons lemon juice
2 tablespoons butter
2 teaspoons shallot, minced
¾ cup Hollandaise Sauce *(page 22)*
2 teaspoons Dijon mustard
8 thin slices Virginia Ham *(page 66)*

Preheat the oven to 450° F.

Place the patty shells upside down on an ungreased baking sheet. Reduce the heat to 400° F. and bake for 20 minutes.

Cut each shell in half, cutting away the sides so that a flat crouton is left. Brown the croutons lightly. Reserve.

Pick over the crabmeat. Discard any bits of shell or cartilage. Toss the crabmeat gently with the lemon juice.

Melt the butter in a small skillet. Add the shallot and sauté over medium heat until soft. Do not brown.

Add the crabmeat and sauté over low heat for 2 minutes, tossing gently so that the crabmeat is well coated with butter.

Combine the Hollandaise Sauce and mustard.

Place 2 croutons on each of 4 warmed plates. Place a slice of Virginia Ham on each crouton and top with the crabmeat. Cover the crabmeat with the Hollandaise Sauce.

BROCCOLI POLONAISE

(4 servings)

In his *Treatise on Gardening*, attorney general John Randolph of Williamsburg gave explicit directions for preparing "brocoli." The mid-eighteenth-century cook was instructed to trim and peel the stems, then boil the broccoli "in a clean cloth" and "serve them up with butter . . . the stems will eat like Asparagus, and the heads like Cauliflower."

1 pound broccoli
¼ cup butter, divided
¼ cup fine bread crumbs
1 tablespoon lemon juice
1 hard-cooked egg, sieved
salt and white pepper

Peel the broccoli and cut an "X" in the base of each stem. Boil or steam the broccoli until tender.

Melt 1 tablespoon of butter in a small skillet. Add the bread crumbs and sauté until golden brown. Reserve.

Melt 3 tablespoons of butter in a small saucepan. Add the lemon juice.

Pour the hot butter over the cooked broccoli. Top with the sieved hard-cooked egg and reserved crumbs.

Add salt and white pepper to taste.

MOCHA MOUSSE

(4 servings)

2 teaspoons instant coffee
2 teaspoons cold water
4 ounces semisweet chocolate
3 eggs, separated
2 tablespoons brandy
1 tablespoon Cointreau
⅓ cup whipping cream
1 tablespoon confectioners' sugar
4 candied violets or *chocolate sprinkles (optional)*

Dissolve the instant coffee in the cold water.

Melt the chocolate in the top of a double boiler over hot water. Add the coffee.

Beat the egg yolks well. Add to the chocolate mixture. Cook, stirring constantly, for 3 minutes.

Add the brandy and Cointreau and cook, stirring constantly, until the mixture starts to thicken. Remove from the heat.

Beat the egg whites until stiff peaks form. Fold them into the chocolate mixture.

Pour into sherbet or wine glasses.

Refrigerate overnight.

Whip the cream until stiff. Add the confectioners' sugar.

Place the sweetened whipped cream in a pastry bag fitted with a decorative tip. Make swirls of whipped cream on top of each serving.

Garnish with a candied violet or chocolate sprinkles if desired.

Seafood at
Christiana Campbell's Tavern

for 6

Honeydew Melon and Cantaloupe Wrapped with
Virginia Ham

*Chesapeake Bay Jambalaya

Okra

Steamed Rice

*Pumpkin Fritters

*Pears and Port Wine

Chesapeake Bay jambalaya is a specialty at Christiana Campbell's, a tavern frequented by George Washington, who often noted in his diary that he had "dined," "supped," or "spent the evening at Mrs. Campbell's," where he enjoyed hearty food and drink served by one of Williamsburg's most renowned hostesses.

CHESAPEAKE BAY JAMBALAYA

(6 servings)

3 tablespoons vegetable oil
½ cup celery, diced
½ cup leek, diced
¾ cup onion, coarsely chopped
½ cup green pepper, coarsely chopped
2 cups Fish Stock *(page 71)* or *1 bottle (8 ounces) clam juice and 1 cup water*
1 clove garlic, minced
1 cup tomato purée
1 cup plum tomatoes, drained and chopped
¼ teaspoon sage
2 teaspoons cornstarch
¼ cup white wine
salt and pepper
1 pound shrimp, cooked, shelled, and deveined
2 tablespoons gumbo filé powder
1 pint oysters, drained
okra
steamed rice

Heat the oil in a saucepan. Add the celery, leek, onion, and green pepper and sauté over medium heat until the vegetables are tender. Do not brown.

Add the Fish Stock and simmer, covered, for 20 minutes. Remove the vegetables. Reserve.

Add the garlic, tomato purée, tomatoes, and sage to the stock. Simmer, covered, for 45 minutes.

Combine the cornstarch and wine. Add to the sauce. Bring to a boil.

Add the reserved vegetables. Season to taste with salt and pepper. Remove from the heat.

Cool completely.

Let stand for several hours, covered, to bring out the flavor.

Just before serving, add the shrimp and gumbo filé powder and reheat the jambalaya.

Add the oysters. Cook just until the edges curl.

Garnish with cooked okra.

Serve over steamed rice.

PUMPKIN FRITTERS

(15–16 fritters)

Apple, raspberry, tansy, parsnip, clary, and plum are some of the other kinds of fritters for which recipes are given in colonial cookery books. The fritters were seasoned and fried much like their modern counterparts, but the ale and dry white wine that eighteenth-century cooks included have been eliminated from the recipe below.

1 egg
½ cup sugar
½ cup light brown sugar
¼ teaspoon salt
½ teaspoon cinnamon
¼ teaspoon nutmeg
½ teaspoon vanilla
1 cup all-purpose flour
1 cup canned or *cooked fresh pumpkin, well drained*
¼ teaspoon baking powder
vegetable oil
confectioners' sugar

Beat the egg, sugars, and salt until light and fluffy.

Add the cinnamon, nutmeg, and vanilla. Mix well.

Add the flour and pumpkin. Mix well. Add the baking powder.

Refrigerate the batter for at least 2 hours.

Drop by tablespoonfuls into deep hot fat (375° F.) and fry for 3 minutes. When the fritters rise to the top, turn them over.

Drain on paper towels.

Sprinkle with confectioners' sugar before serving.

PEARS AND PORT WINE

(6 servings)

6 pears
¾ cup sugar
1 slice lemon
⅛ teaspoon nutmeg
1 2-inch stick of cinnamon
½ cup water
port wine

Choose pears of equal size and shape.

Core the pears from the bottom. Peel, leaving the stems on. If the bottoms are uneven, trim them so that the pears will stand upright.

Combine the sugar, lemon slice, nutmeg, cinnamon stick, and water in a deep, straight-sided glass, stainless steel, or enamel saucepan. Stand the pears upright in the pan. Add enough port wine to cover them by ½ inch. Bring slowly to a boil, reduce the heat, and simmer, covered, for 1 hour.

Place the pears in a glass bowl. Strain the sauce over them.

Refrigerate overnight.

Holiday

Easter at the Williamsburg Lodge

for 6

*Consommé Virginian

*Roast Capon with

*Sage Dressing

*White Wine Sauce

*Green Beans and Zucchini

Mushroom and Spinach Salad

*Lemon-Olive Oil Dressing

*Coconut Cream Pie

CONSOMMÉ VIRGINIAN

(6 servings)

6 cups Clear Consommé *(page 95)*
6 tablespoons dry sherry
2 tablespoons Virginia Ham *(page 66), minced*

Heat the Clear Consommé almost to the boiling point. Add the sherry.

Place 1 teaspoon of minced Virginia Ham in the bottom of each of 6 warmed bouillon cups. Pour the Clear Consommé over the Virginia Ham.

ROAST CAPON

1 6- to 7-pound capon
salt and pepper
Sage Dressing *(below)*
butter
White Wine Sauce *(page 103)*

Preheat the oven to 325° F.

Let the capon stand at room temperature while the dressing is being made.

Wipe the capon inside and out with paper towels.

Sprinkle the cavity with salt and pepper. Stuff the capon with Sage Dressing. Truss the capon. Rub the capon with butter and sprinkle with salt and pepper.

Place the capon, breast up, on a rack in a roasting pan and roast at 325° F. for approximately 2¼ to 2½ hours or until the internal temperature reaches 180° F. Baste occasionally.

Serve with White Wine Sauce.

SAGE DRESSING

(5 cups)

¼ cup butter
¼ cup onion, chopped
¼ cup celery, minced
5 cups stale white bread cubes, lightly toasted
1 teaspoon salt
⅛ teaspoon pepper
1½ teaspoons poultry seasoning
1 egg
½ cup water

Melt the butter in a large heavy skillet. Add the onion and celery and sauté over medium heat until the onion is soft. Do not brown.

Add the bread cubes and toss until they are well combined with the vegetables.

Add the salt, pepper, and poultry seasoning. Toss for 1 minute. Remove from the heat.

Beat the egg and water together. Add to the stuffing mixture.

Stuff and truss the capon.

Place any leftover dressing in a buttered casserole. Bake in the oven with the capon for the last 30 minutes of the roasting time.

WHITE WINE SAUCE

(1¼ cups)

¾ cup dry white wine
½ cup water
2 tablespoons butter

Remove all of the fat from the roasting pan, leaving the drippings.

Add the white wine and water and bring to a boil, stirring with a fork to deglaze the bottom of the pan. Boil for 1 minute. Remove from the heat.

Add the butter.

Strain into a warmed sauceboat.

Modern cooks would agree with Mrs. Glasse's "directions concerning garden things" in which she emphasized that vegetables should be cooked just until tender: "Most people spoil garden things by over-boiling them. All things that are green should have a little crispness, for if they are over-boiled they neither have any sweetness or beauty."

GREEN BEANS AND ZUCCHINI

(6 servings)

1 pound string beans
2 small zucchini
⅓ cup Chicken Stock *(page 30)* or *canned chicken broth*
2 tablespoons butter
2 tablespoons parsley, chopped
¼ teaspoon marjoram
salt and pepper

Cook the string beans in boiling salted water until tender. Drain. Rinse with cold water. Dry on paper towels.

Cut the zucchini in half horizontally. Slice the halves into julienne strips about 2 to 3 inches long.

Heat the Chicken Stock in a skillet. Add the zucchini and cook, stirring constantly, just until tender. Drain.

Melt the butter in a skillet. Add the string beans and zucchini and toss over medium heat until heated through.

Add the parsley, marjoram, and salt and pepper to taste.

LEMON–OLIVE OIL DRESSING

(see page 84)

COCONUT CREAM PIE

¼ cup cornstarch
1 tablespoon flour
3 cups half and half, divided
3 eggs
3 egg yolks
¾ cup sugar
2 teaspoons vanilla
1½ cups flaked coconut, divided
1 9-inch baked Pie Shell *(page 40)*
1 cup whipping cream
2 tablespoons confectioners' sugar

Combine the cornstarch, flour, and ½ cup of half and half. Stir until the cornstarch and flour dissolve.

Beat the eggs, egg yolks, and sugar until light and fluffy.

Heat 2½ cups of half and half to the boiling point. Add the cornstarch mixture.

Gradually pour the hot half and half over the egg mixture, beating constantly.

Cook over medium heat, stirring constantly, until thick. Remove from the heat.

Add the vanilla and 1 cup of coconut.

Cool completely.

When the filling is cold, spoon it into the Pie Shell.

Whip the cream until stiff. Add the confectioners' sugar.

Spread the sweetened whipped cream over the filling. Sprinkle with ½ cup of coconut.

Refrigerate overnight.

Mother's Day Celebration at the Williamsburg Inn

for 6

*Cream of Watercress Soup

*Roast Leg of Lamb with

*Tarragon Sauce

Pan Roasted Potatoes

Buttered Asparagus Spears

Hard Rolls

*Regency Hazelnut Ice Cream Cake

*Chocolate Sauce

CREAM OF WATERCRESS SOUP

(6 servings)

1 bunch watercress
2 tablespoons butter
2 medium potatoes, thinly sliced
¼ cup water
2 cups CHICKEN STOCK *(page 30)* or *canned chicken broth*
2 cups milk
1 cup whipping cream
salt and white pepper

Reserve a few watercress leaves for garnish. Chop the rest of the watercress coarsely.

Melt the butter in a heavy saucepan. Add the watercress, potatoes, and water. Simmer, covered, over low heat for 20 minutes.

Add the Chicken Stock and milk. Bring to a boil, reduce the heat, and simmer, covered, for 20 minutes.

Purée the soup in a food processor or blender.

Return to the heat and add the cream. Do not boil.

Add salt and white pepper to taste.

Garnish with the reserved watercress leaves.

ROAST LEG OF LAMB

1 5- to 6-pound leg of lamb
1 clove garlic, thinly sliced
butter
salt and pepper
TARRAGON SAUCE *(page 107)*
1 teaspoon butter

Ask the butcher to leave the bone end of the leg of lamb intact.

Preheat the oven to 350° F.

Remove as much of the fat as possible. Make little incisions in the leg. Insert the slices of garlic. Rub the lamb with butter and sprinkle with salt and pepper.

Place the lamb on a rack in a roasting pan and roast at 350° F. for approximately 20 minutes per pound or until the internal temperature reaches 140° F. for medium rare. Transfer the lamb to a platter. Keep warm.

Remove all of the fat from the roasting pan, leaving the drippings.

Add the Tarragon Sauce and bring to a boil, stirring with a fork to deglaze the bottom of the pan. Taste for seasoning.

Strain into a warmed sauceboat.

Add the butter.

TARRAGON SAUCE

(2 cups)

1 cup dry white wine
2 teaspoons dried tarragon
2 teaspoons shallot, chopped
1½ cups Beef Stock *(page 35)* or *canned beef bouillon*

Combine the wine and tarragon. Bring to a boil, reduce the heat, and simmer, covered, for 10 minutes.

Add the shallot and Beef Stock and simmer, uncovered, for 5 minutes.

REGENCY HAZELNUT ICE CREAM CAKE

1¾ cups hazelnuts
4 egg yolks
2 cups sugar
½ teaspoon salt
¼ cup flour
8 cups light cream
2½ teaspoons vanilla, divided
½ teaspoon almond extract
Spongecake *(page 79)*
Hazelnut Meringue *(page 108)*
1 cup whipping cream
2 tablespoons confectioners' sugar

Preheat the oven to 350° F.

Bake the hazelnuts at 350° F. for 15 to 20 minutes. Cover and let stand for 10 minutes. Rub the nuts between palms of hands or in a towel to remove the thin skins. Grind the nuts in a food processor or blender. Reserve.

Beat the egg yolks, sugar, salt, and flour until well blended.

Scald the cream. Gradually pour it over the egg mixture, beating constantly.

Cook over medium heat, stirring constantly, until the mixture thickens. Do not let the mixture boil. Remove from the heat.

Add 2 teaspoons of vanilla and the almond extract.

Fold in the hazelnuts.

Pour the mixture into the freezer container of an electric ice cream maker.

Chill thoroughly.

Follow the manufacturer's directions for freezing.

Remove from the freezer and let soften for 10 minutes before placing on the cake.

Freeze the Spongecake for 10 minutes. Slice the Spongecake in half horizontally. Place 1 half on a cake plate. Reserve the other half for another use.

Place the ice cream on top of the cake. The ice cream should be about 2½ inches thick. The sides should be straight and the top as flat as possible.

Place the Hazelnut Meringue on top of the ice cream. Return to the freezer.

Whip the cream until stiff. Add ½ teaspoon of vanilla and the confectioners' sugar.

Frost the top and sides of the cake with ¾ of the whipped cream.

Place the remaining whipped cream in a pastry bag fitted with a decorative tip. Make rosettes of whipped cream around the top of the cake.

HAZELNUT MERINGUE

1 egg white
pinch of salt
¼ cup sugar
2 tablespoons hazelnuts, ground

Preheat the oven to 250° F.

Trace a 10-inch circle on a piece of parchment paper. Place the paper on a baking sheet.

Beat the egg white until frothy. Add the salt and beat until soft peaks form.

Gradually add the sugar, beating until stiff peaks form.

Fold in the hazelnuts.

Place the meringue in the center of the parchment circle. Smooth it evenly to the outer edge with a small spatula.

Bake at 250° F. for 30 minutes. Turn off the oven for 1 hour, leaving the meringue in the oven. Turn on the oven again to 250° F. and bake for an additional 30 minutes. Turn off the oven. Let the meringue remain in the oven without opening the door for at least 2 hours.

CHOCOLATE SAUCE

(see page 80)

Thanksgiving Dinner in Tidewater Virginia

for 12

* Corn Bisque

Roast Young Tom Turkey, Giblet Gravy

*Oyster Dressing

*Cranberry and Orange Relish

*Honey and Cinnamon–Candied Yams

*Green Beans with Surry County Peanuts

*Pumpkin Muffins

*Virginia Apple Custard Tart

Turkey for Thanksgiving is as American as apple pie, a variation of which also appears on this menu. Thanksgiving has traditionally been the time for giving thanks for Nature's bounty and for welcoming family and friends with the legendary Virginia hospitality that has been associated with the Old Dominion since colonial days. "No people can entertain their friends with better cheer and welcome; and strangers and travellers are here treated in the most free, plentiful, and hospitable manner."

CORN BISQUE

(12 servings)

3 cans (17 ounces each) cream style corn
1 medium onion
1 rib of celery
2 cups CHICKEN STOCK *(page 30)* or *canned chicken broth*
4 cups milk, divided
¼ cup butter
¼ cup flour
1 tablespoon steak sauce
1 teaspoon celery salt
Tabasco sauce
salt and white pepper
1 cup whipping cream

Purée the corn, onion, and celery in a food processor or blender. Pour into the top of a double boiler.

Add the Chicken Stock and 3 cups of milk and cook, covered, over boiling water for 45 minutes.

Melt the butter in a saucepan. Stir in the flour and cook over medium heat for 3 minutes, stirring constantly. Do not let the mixture brown.

Heat 1 cup of milk and add it to the butter and flour mixture, whisking until the mixture is smooth and thick. Add the steak sauce, celery salt, and a dash of Tabasco sauce.

Force the corn mixture through a food mill or sieve to remove all fibers.

Return the corn mixture to the double boiler and whisk in the cream sauce.

Add salt and white pepper to taste.

Heat until very hot.

Whip the cream until stiff.

Garnish with the whipped cream.

OYSTER DRESSING

(16 cups)

1 cup butter
1½ cups onion, chopped
1½ cups celery, chopped
2 tablespoons parsley, chopped
1 teaspoon salt
¾ teaspoon pepper
2 tablespoons poultry seasoning
16 cups stale white bread cubes, lightly toasted
1 quart oysters

Melt the butter in a large heavy skillet. Add the onion, celery, and parsley and sauté over medium heat until the vegetables are tender. Do not brown.

Add the salt, pepper, and poultry seasoning. Cook over low heat, stirring constantly, for 2 minutes.

Place the bread cubes in a large bowl. Add the sautéed vegetables. Mix well.

Drain the oysters on paper towels, reserving the liquid. Chop the oysters coarsely. Add to the mixture, tossing gently to mix well. Add a little of the reserved oyster liquid if the dressing seems too dry.

Taste for seasoning.

Stuff and truss the turkey.

Place any leftover dressing in a buttered casserole. Bake in the oven with the turkey for the last 30 minutes of the roasting time.

CRANBERRY AND ORANGE RELISH

(3 cups)

2 cups cranberries
1 orange, quartered and seeded
½ lemon, seeded
1 cup sugar
1 cup pecans
¼ cup Cointreau

Chop the cranberries, orange, and lemon in a food processor.

Add the sugar, pecans, and Cointreau. Process briefly.

Cover and let stand at room temperature for 12 hours.

Refrigerate overnight.

HONEY AND CINNAMON-CANDIED YAMS

(12 servings)

6 large yams
1½ tablespoons cornstarch
2 tablespoons cold water
1½ cups honey
½ teaspoon cinnamon
⅛ teaspoon nutmeg
1½ teaspoons lemon rind, grated
2 teaspoons lemon juice
¼ cup orange juice
1 teaspoon salt
6 tablespoons butter

Preheat the oven to 375° F.

Butter a large ovenproof casserole.

Scrub the yams. Cook the yams in boiling salted water until tender. Drain. Rinse with cold water.

Peel the yams and cut them in half lengthwise. Place the yams in the prepared casserole.

Dissolve the cornstarch in the cold water.

Combine the honey, cinnamon, nutmeg, lemon rind, lemon juice, orange juice, and salt in a saucepan. Bring to a boil.

Add the cornstarch mixture. Cook over medium heat, stirring constantly, until the mixture is thick and clear. Remove from the heat.

Add the butter.

Pour the mixture over the yams.

Bake at 375° F. for 15 minutes.

GREEN BEANS WITH SURRY COUNTY PEANUTS

(12 servings)

3 pounds string beans
6 tablespoons butter
½ cup peanuts, finely chopped

Cook the beans in boiling salted water until tender. Drain.

Melt the butter in a large skillet. Add the beans and peanuts and toss over medium heat until heated through.

PUMPKIN MUFFINS

(2 dozen)

½ cup butter
1 cup sugar
2 eggs
1 cup pumpkin
1 cup raisins
3½ cups all-purpose flour, divided
4 teaspoons baking powder
½ teaspoon cinnamon
½ teaspoon nutmeg
1 teaspoon salt
1¼ cups milk

Preheat the oven to 400° F.

Grease muffin tins that are 2½ inches in diameter.

Cream the butter and sugar until light and fluffy. Beat in the eggs and pumpkin.

Dredge the raisins with ½ cup of flour.

Sift 3 cups of flour and the baking powder, cinnamon, nutmeg, and salt together.

Add the dry ingredients and milk alternately by hand, mixing just until blended. Do not overmix.

Add the raisins.

Spoon into the prepared muffin tins, filling each tin ¾ full.
Bake at 400° F. for 20 to 25 minutes.

VIRGINIA APPLE CUSTARD TART

PASTRY *(page 53)*
3 to 4 medium cooking apples
lemon juice
SPONGECAKE *(page 79)*
VANILLA CREAM CUSTARD *(page 74)*
½ cup apricot jam, forced through a sieve
1 tablespoon sugar
2 tablespoons kirsch
¼ cup sliced almonds, toasted

Preheat the oven to 375° F.

Lightly oil a 10-inch tart pan that is 1½ inches deep.

Roll out the Pastry ⅛ inch thick on a lightly floured board or pastry cloth. Press it firmly into the prepared pan. Prick the dough well with a fork. Place greased waxed paper over the dough and fill with dried beans to prevent the dough from rising.

Bake at 375° F. for 35 minutes. Remove from the oven, empty the beans, prick the bottom, and return to the oven for 5 minutes or until the shell is golden brown.

Cool completely.

Line a baking sheet with aluminum foil.

Quarter, peel, and core the apples. Brush the apple quarters with lemon juice to keep them from discoloring.

Make 5 shallow vertical cuts down the back of each apple quarter. Be sure the cuts are shallow so that the quarters will hold their shape as they bake.

Arrange the apple quarters, cored side down, on the prepared baking sheet.

Bake at 375° F. for 15 minutes or until the apples are tender.

Cool completely.

Slice the Spongecake in half horizontally. Place 1 half in the tart shell.

Spread the Vanilla Cream Custard on top of the Spongecake.

Arrange the apple quarters in a circle on top of the Vanilla Cream Custard. Slightly overlap 3 apple quarters in the center.

Refrigerate.

Shortly before serving, combine the apricot jam and sugar in a small saucepan. Bring to a boil, stirring constantly. Remove from the heat.

Cool slightly before adding the kirsch.

Brush the rim of the tart with the glaze. Press on the almonds.

Spoon the rest of the glaze over the top of the tart.

Holiday Cocktail Supper

for 25

*Vegetable Pinwheel with

*Bleu Cheese Dip *or*

*Curry Mayonnaise

*Marinated Mushrooms

*Cheddar Cheese and Bacon Balls

*Meatballs in
*Sweet and Sour Sauce

*Roast Marinated Tenderloin of Beef
*Horseradish Cream

Rye Bread Rounds

*Baked Brie

*Party Fruit Bowl

VEGETABLE PINWHEEL

Use an assortment of vegetables in season such as carrots, celery, zucchini, green beans, asparagus, mushrooms, green onions, cherry tomatoes, radishes, or green peppers.

Arrange the vegetables attractively on a large platter.

Place a bowl of dip in the center.

BLEU CHEESE DIP

(3½ cups)

4 ounces bleu cheese
8 ounces cream cheese
½ cup Parmesan cheese, grated
1 cup sour cream
1 cup MAYONNAISE *(page 43)*
2 teaspoons soy sauce

Combine the bleu cheese and cream cheese. Beat until well blended.

Add the Parmesan, sour cream, Mayonnaise, and soy sauce. Mix well.

Refrigerate overnight.

CURRY MAYONNAISE

(1¼ cups)

1¼ cups MAYONNAISE *(page 43)*
1 teaspoon curry powder
1 clove garlic, pressed
Tabasco sauce

Combine the Mayonnaise, curry powder, garlic, and 4 drops of Tabasco sauce. Mix well.

Chill thoroughly.

MARINATED MUSHROOMS

(4 cups)

½ cup olive oil
2 pounds small whole mushrooms
1 tablespoon white wine vinegar
1 tablespoon lemon juice
½ teaspoon salt
½ teaspoon garlic powder
⅛ teaspoon white pepper
½ teaspoon oregano
½ teaspoon basil
½ teaspoon thyme

Heat the oil in a heavy skillet. Add the mushrooms and sauté over medium heat for 2 to 3 minutes.

Place the mushrooms in a bowl. Add the vinegar, lemon juice, salt, garlic powder, white pepper, oregano, basil, and thyme. Mix well.

Refrigerate overnight.

Drain well before serving.

CHEDDAR CHEESE AND BACON BALLS

(4 dozen)

4 slices lean bacon
¼ pound Cheddar cheese, grated
¼ cup butter
⅛ teaspoon cayenne
¾ cup all-purpose flour

Preheat the oven to 375° F. 10 minutes before the cheese and bacon balls are ready to be baked.

The cheese and butter should be at room temperature.

Fry the bacon until it is very crisp. Drain well. Crumble the bacon. Reserve.

Combine the cheese, butter, and cayenne.

Add the flour. Mix well, by hand, until the mixture is smooth and deep yellow in color.

Cover and let stand at room temperature for 15 minutes.

Pinch off small pieces of dough (about 1 teaspoon) and flatten in palm of hand to a circle about 1 inch in diameter.

Place a few bits of crumbled bacon in the center of the dough. Bring the edges together to cover the bacon completely. Roll gently between palms of hands.

Place on an ungreased baking sheet.

Chill in the refrigerator for 10 minutes.

Bake at 375° F. for 15 minutes or until lightly browned.

Serve hot.

MEATBALLS IN SWEET AND SOUR SAUCE

(125 meatballs)

2 medium potatoes
3 slices stale bread
1½ pounds hamburger
½ pound sausage
1 medium onion, finely chopped
2 eggs, lightly beaten
2 teaspoons salt
½ teaspoon pepper
½ teaspoon allspice
½ teaspoon nutmeg
2 tablespoons butter
2 tablespoons vegetable oil
4 cups BEEF STOCK *(page 35)* or *canned beef bouillon*
SWEET AND SOUR SAUCE *(page 117)*

Christmas Dinner in Williamsburg begins with a smooth, flavorful Duck Pâté. The soup is a tureen of Lobster Bisque Chantilly, rich with bits of lobster and lightly seasoned with sherry. The main course, consisting of Baked Sugar Cured Ham and Braised Belgian Endive, is followed by Grapefruit Ice to clear and refresh the palate. A blazing Plum Pudding served with Brandied Hard Sauce brings the gala feast to an exciting conclusion. ►

Preheat the oven to 300° F.

Cook the potatoes in boiling salted water until tender. Drain, reserving the water.

Crumble the bread into the bowl of an electric mixer. Add ½ cup of the potato water and beat until mushy. Add the potatoes and beat until well blended.

Add the hamburger, sausage, onion, eggs, salt, pepper, allspice, and nutmeg. Beat for 4 minutes. Add a little more potato water if the mixture seems too dry.

Heat the butter and oil in a large heavy skillet.

Roll half-tablespoonfuls of the mixture between palms of hands and drop them into the hot fat. Shake the skillet so that the meatballs brown lightly on all sides. Transfer the browned meatballs to a roasting pan. Repeat the process until all of the meatball mixture has been used.

Add the Beef Stock to the roasting pan. Cover with aluminum foil.

Bake at 300° F. for 1 hour.

Transfer the meatballs to a chafing dish.

Add 1 cup of the cooking liquid to the Sweet and Sour Sauce. Pour the sauce over the meatballs.

Serve hot.

SWEET AND SOUR SAUCE

(2 cups)

3 slices lean bacon
2 cups raspberry or *white wine vinegar*
¾ cup sugar
½ cup apple juice
¼ cup apples, diced
¼ teaspoon cinnamon
1 small bay leaf
2 cloves
1 small clove garlic, pressed
Tabasco sauce
3 tablespoons arrowroot
2 tablespoons cold water
salt and pepper

Fry the bacon until it is very crisp. Drain well. Crumble the bacon. Reserve.

Add the vinegar, sugar, apple juice, apples, cinnamon, bay leaf, cloves, garlic, and 4 to 6 drops of Tabasco sauce to the fat left in the skillet. Simmer, uncovered, for 20 minutes. Discard the bay leaf and cloves.

Dissolve the arrowroot in the cold water. Add to the sauce. Cook over medium heat, stirring constantly, until the sauce thickens.

Add the crumbled bacon.

Add salt and pepper to taste.

◄ *A Viennese Chocolate Torte and Sparkling Champagne are a fitting climax to a New Year's Eve Collation that bids farewell to the year just past and welcomes the one to come.*

ROAST MARINATED TENDERLOIN OF BEEF

1 3-pound tenderloin of beef, trimmed
MARINADE *(below)*
HORSERADISH CREAM *(below)*
Dijon mustard
rye bread rounds

Tie the tenderloin so that it will keep its shape.

Place the tenderloin in a non-metal container. Pour the Marinade over the meat. Refrigerate and let stand for 24 hours, turning the meat occasionally.

Preheat the oven to 425° F.

Remove the meat from the Marinade. Wipe it dry with paper towels.

Place the tenderloin on a rack in a roasting pan and roast at 425° F. for approximately 20 to 25 minutes per pound or until the internal temperature reaches 125° F. for rosy rare. Cool to room temperature.

Slice the meat thinly.

Serve with Horseradish Cream, Dijon mustard, and rye bread rounds.

MARINADE

(3 cups)

¼ cup olive oil
2½ cups red Burgundy wine
½ cup onion, chopped
½ cup carrot, chopped
2 teaspoons salt
3 peppercorns
3 cloves
¼ teaspoon thyme
1 bay leaf

Combine the olive oil, wine, onion, carrot, salt, peppercorns, cloves, thyme, and bay leaf. Mix well.

HORSERADISH CREAM

(1 cup)

1 cup whipping cream
¼ cup prepared horseradish
¾ teaspoon salt

Whip the cream until stiff.

Fold in the prepared horseradish and salt.

Refrigerate overnight.

BAKED BRIE

1 2-pound brie, chilled
salt
slivered almonds
1 tablespoon butter, melted
crackers

Preheat the oven to 300° F. 10 minutes before the brie is to be baked.

Cut a circle on the top of the brie. Leave a rim of about ½ inch. Remove the rind from the circle so that the top center is exposed. Sprinkle the top lightly with salt and cover with slivered almonds.

Cover the brie with plastic wrap and let it stand at room temperature for ½ hour or until the inside is soft.

Brush with melted butter.

Bake at 300° F. for 10 minutes.

Use a spoon to spread the melted brie on crackers. Be careful not to cut into the rind.

PARTY FRUIT BOWL

(16 cups)

Rare and expensive, the pineapple, which became the colonial symbol of hospitality, was discovered in the New World and imported to Europe in the sixteenth century where some were grown in hothouses. George Washington tasted it in Barbados in 1751, noting that of all the exotic fruits, "none pleases my taste as do's the Pine." A pineapple is carved over a doorway at William Byrd's Westover plantation on the James River; others were used there as finials on fence posts.

1 large ripe pineapple
2 large honeydew melons
2 large cantaloupes
1 can (6 ounces) frozen lemonade concentrate

Remove the top of the pineapple. Peel and core the pineapple and cut it into chunks.

Cut the melons into balls with a melon ball cutter.

Combine the lemonade concentrate and 1½ cans of cold water. Mix well. Pour over the fruit.

Chill thoroughly.

Drain the fruit and arrange it in a glass bowl.

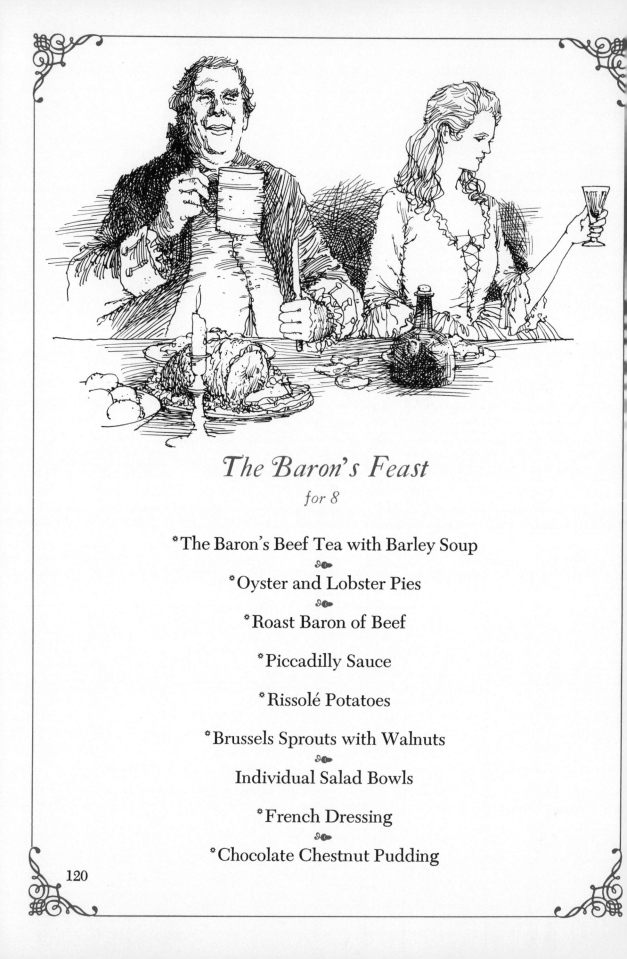

The Baron's Feast

for 8

*The Baron's Beef Tea with Barley Soup

*Oyster and Lobster Pies

*Roast Baron of Beef

*Piccadilly Sauce

*Rissolé Potatoes

*Brussels Sprouts with Walnuts

Individual Salad Bowls

*French Dressing

*Chocolate Chestnut Pudding

The hearty good cheer so typical of Christmas in colonial Virginia has been re-created at the Baron's Feast. Everyone joins in the revels, which feature a lavish five-course meal and rollicking entertainment.

THE BARON'S BEEF TEA WITH BARLEY SOUP

(8 servings)

5 veal bones
1 pound stewing beef
3 ribs of celery, chopped
2 medium onions, chopped
⅛ teaspoon oregano
Worcestershire sauce
16 cups water
salt and pepper
½ cup barley

Preheat the oven to 400° F.

Place the veal bones and stewing beef in a roasting pan and brown in the oven at 400° F. for 45 minutes or until well browned.

Remove from the oven, drain the fat, and place the bones in a soup pot. Add the celery, onions, oregano, a dash of Worcestershire sauce, and the water. Bring to a boil, reduce the heat, and simmer, uncovered, for 1½ hours, removing any scum that appears on the surface.

Strain the stock and remove all fat.

Add salt and pepper to taste.

Add the barley and simmer for 30 minutes or until the barley is tender.

OYSTER AND LOBSTER PIES

(8 servings)

Although some ingredients—pistachios and marrow, for example—that appeared in eighteenth-century recipes for oyster and lobster pies are no longer in vogue, the pies themselves have remained popular. Mrs. Raffald announced in her cookery book that a "Lobster Pye" was considered "a genteel corner dish for a dinner."

10 tablespoons butter, divided
6 tablespoons flour
1¾ cups Fish Stock *(page 71)* or *1 bottle (8 ounces) clam juice and ¾ cup water*
¼ cup dry white wine
11 ounces lobster meat, diced
½ pound mushrooms, thinly sliced
1 pint oysters, drained
2 teaspoons lemon juice
½ cup Amontillado sherry
salt and white pepper
Pastry Topping *(page 122)*
1 egg yolk
1 teaspoon water

Preheat the oven to 400° F. 10 minutes before the oyster and lobster pies are ready to be baked.

Butter 8 individual casseroles or shirred egg dishes.

Melt 4 tablespoons of butter in a saucepan. Stir in the flour and cook over medium heat for 3 minutes, stirring constantly. Do not let the mixture brown.

Heat the Fish Stock and add it to the mixture, whisking until the mixture is smooth and thick.

Add the white wine. Bring to a boil, reduce the heat, and simmer, partially covered, for 20 minutes.

Melt 2 tablespoons of butter in a large skillet. Add the lobster meat and sauté over medium heat for 2 minutes. Add the lobster meat to the sauce.

Melt 4 tablespoons of butter in the skillet. Add the mushrooms and sauté over medium heat until they are almost dry. Add the mushrooms to the sauce.

Add the oysters, lemon juice, sherry, and salt and white pepper to taste.

Pour into the prepared casseroles.

For easy handling, work with only ¼ of the Pastry Topping at a time. Keep the rest refrigerated until ready to roll out.

Roll out the dough ⅛ inch thick on a lightly floured board or pastry cloth. Place a plate that is slightly larger in diameter than the shirred egg dishes on top of the pastry and cut 2 circles from each portion with a sharp knife.

Top each casserole with a circle of pastry, sealing the edges to the rim. Prick the pastry with a fork.

Beat the egg yolk and water together until well blended. Brush the pastry with the egg glaze.

Bake at 400° F. for 30 minutes.

PASTRY TOPPING

(8 servings)

3 cups all-purpose flour
1 teaspoon salt
1 cup vegetable shortening
1 egg
½ cup ice water

Combine the flour and salt. Mix well.

Cut in the shortening with knives or a pastry blender until the mixture is mealy.

Beat the egg lightly. Add the ice water and beat until well blended. Stir into the flour mixture. Mix well.

Wrap the dough in waxed paper. Refrigerate for 30 minutes.

ROAST BARON OF BEEF

1 5-pound tenderloin of beef, trimmed
salt and pepper
PICCADILLY SAUCE *(below)*

Preheat the oven to 425° F.

Sprinkle the beef with salt and pepper.

Place the beef on a rack in a roasting pan and roast at 425° F. for approximately 35 to 45 minutes or until the internal temperature reaches 125° F. for rosy rare.

Let stand for 20 minutes before carving.

Serve with Piccadilly Sauce.

PICCADILLY SAUCE

(3½ cups)

2 tablespoons butter
1 shallot, finely chopped
¼ pound mushrooms, sliced
1 cup tomatoes, drained and chopped
2 cups BEEF STOCK *(page 35)* or *canned beef bouillon*
1 cup CHICKEN STOCK *(page 30)* or *canned chicken broth*
1 teaspoon parsley, chopped
¼ cup dry white wine
⅛ teaspoon freshly ground pepper
1 tablespoon arrowroot
1 tablespoon cold water
salt

Melt the butter in a heavy saucepan. Add the shallot and mushrooms and sauté over medium heat for 8 minutes, stirring frequently.

Add the tomatoes, Beef Stock, Chicken Stock, parsley, wine, and pepper. Bring to a boil, reduce the heat, and simmer, uncovered, for 1 hour.

Dissolve the arrowroot in the cold water. Add to the sauce. Cook over medium heat, stirring constantly, until the sauce thickens.

Add salt to taste.

RISSOLÉ POTATOES

(see page 78)

BRUSSELS SPROUTS WITH WALNUTS

(8 servings)

1¼ pounds Brussels sprouts
½ cup butter
2 tablespoons lemon juice
1 teaspoon dill weed
½ cup walnuts, coarsely chopped
salt and pepper

Trim the Brussels sprouts and cut an "X" in the base of each. Boil or steam the Brussels sprouts until tender.

Melt the butter in a skillet. Add the lemon juice, dill weed, and walnuts and sauté gently for 2 minutes. Do not let the butter brown.

Add the Brussels sprouts and toss over medium heat until heated through.

Add salt and pepper to taste.

FRENCH DRESSING

(see page 43)

CHOCOLATE CHESTNUT PUDDING

(8 servings)

6 ounces semisweet chocolate
1¾ cups milk
½ cup sugar
⅛ teaspoon salt
2 teaspoons vanilla
2 eggs
2 egg yolks
1 can (15½ ounces) chestnut purée
1 cup whipping cream
2 tablespoons confectioners' sugar
candied violets (optional)

Preheat the oven to 350° F.

Butter a 1½-quart soufflé dish.

Combine the chocolate, milk, sugar, and salt in the top of a double boiler. Mix well. Cook over hot water until the chocolate melts. Remove from the heat. Add the vanilla.

Beat the eggs and egg yolks well. Gradually add the chestnut purée, beating until the mixture is smooth.

Gradually add the chocolate mixture to the chestnut mixture, beating constantly.

Pour the pudding into the prepared dish and place it in a pan of hot water on the middle shelf of the oven.

Bake for 60 to 65 minutes.

Cool completely.

Refrigerate overnight.

Whip the cream until stiff. Add the confectioners' sugar.

Garnish with the whipped cream and candied violets if desired.

Note: This pudding is very rich—servings should be small.

Yuletide Supper

for 6

*Christmas Broth

*Boneless Breast of Chicken with Virginia Ham on

*Croutons

*Madeira Sauce

* Duchesse Potatoes

*Artichoke Bottoms, St. Germain

*Eggnog Ice Cream

CHRISTMAS BROTH

(6 servings)

3 cups vegetable tomato juice
2 cups CHICKEN STOCK *(page 30)* or *canned chicken broth*
2 tablespoons light brown sugar
2 tablespoons sherry
2 tablespoons butter
2 tablespoons parsley, finely chopped

Combine the vegetable tomato juice, Chicken Stock, brown sugar, and sherry in the top of a double boiler. Heat almost to the boiling point. Add the butter.

Serve in individual warmed bouillon cups or soup plates.

Sprinkle on the parsley in the shape of a wreath.

BONELESS BREAST OF CHICKEN WITH VIRGINIA HAM

(6 servings)

6 large chicken breasts, skinned and boned
3 tablespoons butter
salt and white pepper
CROUTONS *(below)*
6 thin slices VIRGINIA HAM *(page 66)*
watercress
MADEIRA SAUCE *(page 127)*

Preheat the oven to 400° F.

Trim the chicken breasts attractively.

Melt the butter in a heavy ovenproof casserole with a lid. Add the chicken breasts, tucking the edges under if necessary. Cook the breasts over medium heat for 1 minute. Turn the breasts over and cook for 1 minute.

Sprinkle the chicken breasts with salt and white pepper. Cover with a piece of buttered waxed paper. Put the lid on the casserole.

Bake at 400° F. for 6 minutes or until the chicken breasts are firm to the touch.

Place a Crouton on each of 6 warmed plates. Place a slice of Virginia Ham on each Crouton. Top with a chicken breast.

Garnish with watercress.

Serve with Madeira Sauce.

CROUTONS

(6 servings)

6 slices slightly stale bread
2 tablespoons butter, divided
2 tablespoons vegetable oil, divided

Cut the croutons out of the bread with a 4-inch cutter.

Heat 1 tablespoon of butter and 1 tablespoon of oil in a heavy skillet. Add 3 croutons and brown well on both sides. Reserve.

Add the remaining butter and oil and brown the remaining 3 croutons.

MADEIRA SAUCE

(2 cups)

3 tablespoons unsalted butter, divided
2 tablespoons onion, minced
1 tablespoon carrot, minced
2½ tablespoons flour
2 cups BEEF STOCK *(page 35)* or *canned beef bouillon*
2 large shallots, minced
¼ teaspoon freshly ground pepper
½ cup Madeira

Melt 2 tablespoons of butter in a small heavy saucepan and cook over medium heat until light brown. Add the onion and carrot and sauté over medium heat for 3 minutes. Stir in the flour and cook, stirring frequently, until the mixture is lightly browned.

Heat the Beef Stock and add it to the mixture, whisking until the mixture is smooth and thick. Bring to a boil, reduce the heat, and simmer, covered, for 1 hour.

Melt 1 tablespoon of butter in a small saucepan. Add the shallots and sauté over medium heat until soft. Add the pepper and cook, stirring constantly, for 1 minute.

Add the Madeira and cook over low heat for 10 minutes or until the liquid is reduced by half.

Add the Madeira mixture to the brown sauce and simmer for 12 minutes. Taste for seasoning.

Strain into a warmed sauceboat.

DUCHESSE POTATOES

(6 servings)

3 medium to large potatoes
3 tablespoons butter
2 egg yolks
salt and white pepper
1 egg

Preheat the oven to 400° F.

Butter a baking sheet.

Peel and quarter the potatoes. Cook the potatoes in boiling salted water until tender. Drain. Return the potatoes to the pan and shake over low heat until dry. Force the potatoes through a ricer or mash thoroughly.

Add the butter and egg yolks. Beat well.

Add salt and white pepper to taste.

Place the mixture in a pastry bag fitted with a large decorative tip. Pipe decorative mounds on the prepared baking sheet.

Beat the egg well. Brush each mound with the egg glaze.

Bake at 400° F. for 20 minutes or until golden brown.

ARTICHOKE BOTTOMS, ST. GERMAIN

(6 servings)

1 can (14 ounces) artichoke bottoms
1 cup peas, cooked
butter
salt and white pepper

Drain the artichoke bottoms. Rinse. Dry on paper towels.

Purée the peas. Add butter, salt, and white pepper to taste.

Heat the artichoke bottoms.

Place the puréed peas in a pastry bag fitted with a decorative tip. Fill the centers of the artichokes with puréed peas.

EGGNOG ICE CREAM

(1 quart)

2 egg yolks
1 cup sugar
¼ teaspoon salt
2 tablespoons flour
4 cups light cream
½ teaspoon nutmeg
yellow food coloring
2 tablespoons imitation brandy extract
2 tablespoons imitation rum extract

Beat the egg yolks, sugar, salt, and flour until light and fluffy.

Scald the cream. Gradually pour it over the egg mixture, beating constantly.

Cook over medium heat, stirring constantly, until the mixture thickens. Do not let the mixture boil. Remove from the heat.

Add the nutmeg and a few drops of food coloring.

Pour the mixture into the freezer container of an electric ice cream maker.

Chill thoroughly.

Add the brandy and rum extracts.

Follow the manufacturer's directions for freezing.

Christmas Dinner in Williamsburg

for 8

*Duck Pâté

Melba Toast

*Lobster Bisque Chantilly

Baked Sugar-Cured Ham

*Potato Puffs

*Braised Belgian Endive

*Grapefruit Ice

*Plum Pudding

*Brandied Hard Sauce

For many, Christmas dinner is the culinary highlight of the holiday season. The menu that follows includes some latter-day innovations such as a palate clearing grapefruit ice, but it also hearkens back to the feasts of yesteryear when joints of meat and plum puddings flamed with brandy graced the tables of our forefathers.

DUCK PÂTÉ

(8 servings)

12 tablespoons unsalted butter, divided
1 small onion, minced
½ pound chicken livers
1 duck liver
1 cup Chicken Stock *(page 30)* or *canned chicken broth*
4 hard-cooked eggs
1 cup duck meat, roasted
2 teaspoons Dijon mustard
Tabasco sauce
1 clove garlic, pressed
3 tablespoons brandy
2 tablespoons lemon juice
salt and pepper
¼ pound boiled ham, diced
½ cup pecans, finely ground

Line individual brioche tins or large muffin tins with fluted paper baking cups.

Melt 2 tablespoons of butter in a small skillet. Add the onion and sauté until soft. Reserve.

Simmer the chicken livers and duck liver in the Chicken Stock for 5 minutes. Drain.

Purée the onion, chicken and duck livers, hard-cooked eggs, duck meat, mustard, 6 drops of Tabasco sauce, garlic, brandy, and lemon juice in a food processor or blender for 3 minutes or until absolutely smooth.

Force the pâté through a sieve to remove all fibers.

Season to taste with salt and pepper.

Add 10 tablespoons of butter and purée until completely blended. Add the diced ham.

Fill the cups with the pâté. Refrigerate overnight.

Unmold the pâtés on individual small plates. Top with the finely ground pecans.

LOBSTER BISQUE CHANTILLY

(8 servings)

½ cup butter, divided
½ cup carrot, chopped
½ cup onion, chopped
½ cup flour
6 cups Fish Stock *(page 71)* or *2 bottles (8 ounces each) clam juice and 4 cups* Chicken Stock *(page 30)* or *canned chicken broth*
11 ounces lobster meat, finely chopped
½ cup Amontillado sherry
1 cup light cream
salt and white pepper
red food coloring
1 cup whipping cream
finely minced parsley or *paprika (optional)*

Melt ¼ cup of butter in a heavy saucepan. Add the carrot and onion and sauté over low heat for 5 minutes. Do not brown. Stir in the flour and cook over medium heat, stirring constantly, until the mixture is lightly browned.

Heat the Fish Stock and add it to the mixture, whisking until the mixture is smooth and thick. Simmer for 20 minutes.

Strain the mixture into the top of a double boiler.

Melt ¼ cup of butter in a large skillet. Add the lobster meat and sauté over medium heat for 2 minutes. Add the lobster meat to the soup.

Add the sherry and light cream.

Add salt and white pepper to taste.

Cook, covered, over simmering water for 30 minutes.

Add 2 to 3 drops of food coloring.

Whip the cream until stiff.

Garnish with the whipped cream and a little finely minced parsley or a dash of paprika if desired.

POTATO PUFFS

(3 dozen)

1½ cups potatoes, cubed
½ cup butter, divided
¼ cup milk
salt and white pepper
¾ cup water
½ teaspoon salt
¾ cup flour
3 eggs
vegetable oil

Cook the potatoes in boiling salted water until tender. Drain. Return the potatoes to the pan and shake over low heat until dry. Mash the potatoes thoroughly.

Add 2 tablespoons of butter and the milk. Beat well.

Add salt and white pepper to taste. Reserve.

Combine the water, 6 tablespoons of butter, and ½ teaspoon of salt in a saucepan. Bring to a boil. Add the flour and stir with a wooden spoon over low heat until the dough forms a ball and no longer sticks to the pan. Remove from the heat.

Add the eggs, 1 at a time, beating well after each addition.

Combine the 2 mixtures. Mix well.

Drop by scant tablespoonfuls into deep hot fat (375° F.) and fry for 3 to 5 minutes, turning the potato puffs over to brown evenly. Do not fry more than 5 or 6 puffs at a time.

Drain on paper towels.

The potato puffs may be fried in advance. Reheat in a 425° F. oven for 5 minutes.

BRAISED BELGIAN ENDIVE

(8 servings)

8 Belgian endive
½ cup Chicken Stock *(page 30)* or *canned chicken broth*
1 tablespoon lemon juice
salt and white pepper
1 tablespoon butter

Preheat the oven to 350° F.

Butter a large ovenproof casserole.

Place the endive in the prepared casserole in a single layer.

Add the Chicken Stock, lemon juice, and salt and white pepper to taste. Dot with the butter.

Cover the casserole tightly.

Bake at 350° F. for 30 minutes or until tender, turning the endive over after 15 minutes.

Rapidly reduce the pan juices to 2 tablespoons. Pour over the braised endive.

GRAPEFRUIT ICE

(2 quarts)

2 cups sugar
3 cups water
3 cups fresh grapefruit juice
1 tablespoon grapefruit rind, grated
1 teaspoon lemon rind, grated
½ cup lemon juice

Combine the sugar and water in a saucepan. Bring to a boil, reduce the heat, and simmer, uncovered, for 5 minutes. Cool to lukewarm.

Add the grapefruit juice, grapefruit rind, lemon rind, and lemon juice.

Chill thoroughly.

Strain the mixture into the freezer container of an electric ice cream maker.

Follow the manufacturer's directions for freezing.

PLUM PUDDING

3 cups coarse bread crumbs
1 cup light brown sugar
1½ teaspoons cinnamon
1½ teaspoons nutmeg
¾ teaspoon allspice
½ teaspoon cloves
½ pound suet, finely chopped
½ pound dried currants
½ pound seeded Muscat raisins
½ pound seedless raisins
¼ pound citron, finely cut
¼ pound candied orange peel, finely cut
6 eggs
½ cup white wine
14 tablespoons brandy, divided
Brandied Hard Sauce *(page 133)*

Prepare the plum pudding 4 weeks before Christmas so that it will season properly.

Grease a 2-quart pudding mold.

Combine the bread crumbs, brown sugar, cinnamon, nutmeg, allspice, and cloves. Mix well.

Add the suet. Mix well.

Add the currants, Muscat raisins, seedless raisins, citron, and candied orange peel. Mix well.

Beat the eggs until light.

Add the eggs and white wine. Mix well.

Place the mixture in the prepared mold. Cover tightly.

Place the mold on a trivet in a large kettle. Fill the kettle with enough water to come ⅔ of the way up the sides of the mold. Cover the kettle.

Steam for 6 hours.

Remove the mold from the water bath. Remove the cover from the mold. Cool for 20 minutes. Unmold the pudding. Finish cooling on a rack.

Wash out the mold. Line the mold with plastic wrap.

Wrap the pudding in damp cheesecloth. Replace the pudding in the mold. Prick the pudding with a skewer in several places. Sprinkle with 3 tablespoons of brandy. Repeat this process once a week for 3 weeks. Keep the pudding covered so that it will not dry out.

Before serving, place the covered mold on a trivet in a large kettle. Fill the kettle with enough water to come ⅔ of the way up the sides of the mold. Cover the kettle.

Steam for 3 hours.

Unmold the pudding. Warm 2 tablespoons of brandy and ignite it. Pour the brandy over the pudding and carry it flaming to the table.

Serve with Brandied Hard Sauce.

BRANDIED HARD SAUCE

(1½ cups)

½ cup butter
1½ cups confectioners' sugar
½ teaspoon vanilla
¼ teaspoon almond extract
1 tablespoon brandy
⅛ teaspoon nutmeg

Cream the butter.

Gradually add the confectioners' sugar. Beat well.

Add the vanilla, almond extract, brandy, and nutmeg. Beat well.

Chill thoroughly.

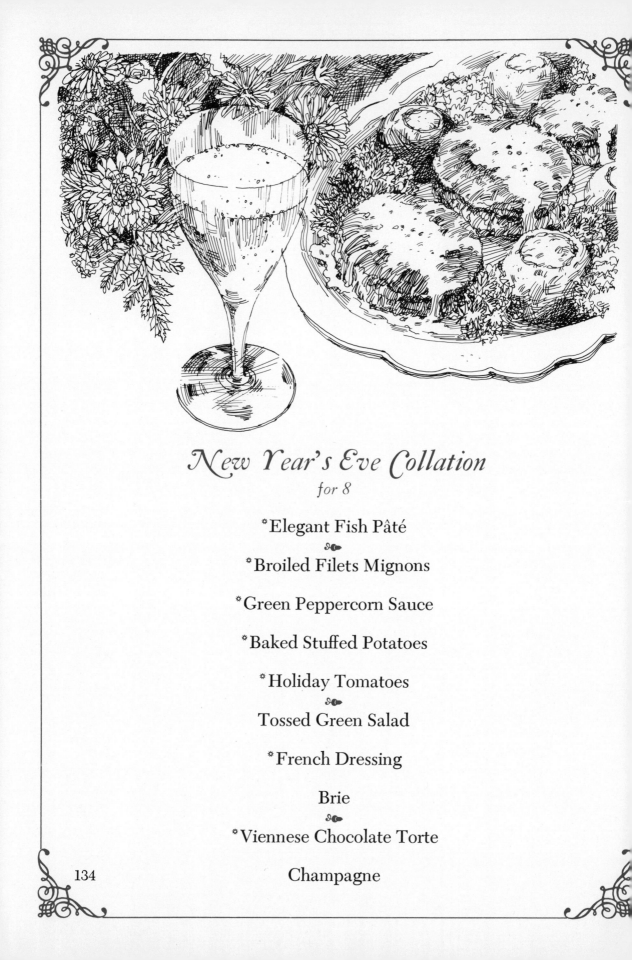

New Year's Eve Collation

for 8

*Elegant Fish Pâté

*Broiled Filets Mignons

*Green Peppercorn Sauce

*Baked Stuffed Potatoes

*Holiday Tomatoes

Tossed Green Salad

*French Dressing

Brie

*Viennese Chocolate Torte

Champagne

New Year's Eve is a time to gather with relatives or close friends and bid farewell to the year just past while welcoming the one to come. The highlight of the meal occurs at the stroke of midnight when a Viennese chocolate torte and sparkling champagne herald the New Year.

ELEGANT FISH PÂTÉ

(8 servings)

1½ pounds white fish fillets, divided
salt and white pepper
⅔ cup dry white wine
10 tablespoons butter, divided
2 tablespoons shallot, chopped
8 cups water
2 cups fresh spinach leaves, packed
2 eggs
⅛ teaspoon nutmeg
1½ pounds fresh salmon or *1 can (15½ ounces) and 1 can (7¾ ounces) red sockeye salmon*
1 teaspoon lemon juice
⅔ cup MAYONNAISE *(page 43)*
⅓ cup sour cream
red lumpfish caviar

Preheat the oven to 275° F.

Butter a 2-quart loaf casserole.

Cut ½ pound of the white fish fillets into strips 2 inches long x ½ inch wide. Place the strips in a ceramic dish. Sprinkle with salt and white pepper. Add the wine.

Melt 1 tablespoon of butter in a small skillet. Add the shallot and sauté over medium heat until soft. Do not brown. Reserve.

Bring the water to a boil. Add the spinach. Bring to a boil and cook for 1 minute. Drain the spinach in a colander. Press out the excess moisture with the back of a wooden spoon.

Purée the spinach in a food processor. Reserve.

Separate 1 egg. Reserve the yolk and white.

Purée the remaining white fish fillets in a food processor until smooth. Add the egg white, 3 tablespoons of butter, 2 teaspoons shallot, ½ teaspoon salt, and ⅛ teaspoon white pepper. Process until well blended. Remove ⅔ of the mixture. Reserve. Add the spinach and nutmeg to the remaining mixture and process until well blended. Reserve.

Purée the salmon in a food processor. Add the egg yolk, egg, lemon juice, remaining shallot, and 6 tablespoons of butter. Process until well blended. Add salt and white pepper to taste.

Drain the fish strips.

Spread ½ of the salmon mixture in the prepared loaf pan. Cover with ⅓ of the fish strips. Cover with the white fish mixture. Cover with ⅓ of the fish strips. Cover with the spinach mixture. Cover with the final ⅓ of the fish strips. Cover with the remaining salmon mixture.

Cover with a double thickness of aluminum foil.

Place the dish in a roasting pan. Fill the pan with enough hot water to come ⅔ of the way up the sides of the dish.

Bake at 275° F. for 2½ hours.

Remove the dish from the water bath.

Cool completely.

Refrigerate overnight.

Combine the Mayonnaise and sour cream. Mix well.

Garnish slices of the fish pâté with dollops of the Mayonnaise–sour cream mixture. Top with the red lumpfish caviar.

BROILED FILETS MIGNONS

(8 servings)

8 filets mignons
8 CROUTONS *(page 126)*
GREEN PEPPERCORN SAUCE *(below)*

Pan broil or grill the filets mignons until done.

Place a Crouton on each of 8 warmed plates. Place a filet mignon on each Crouton. Top with a generous spoonful of Green Peppercorn Sauce.

GREEN PEPPERCORN SAUCE

(¾ cup)

1 tablespoon butter
2 tablespoons shallot, finely chopped
¼ pound mushrooms, finely chopped
2 tablespoons parsley, minced
1 teaspoon green peppercorns, rinsed and drained
Tabasco sauce
2 tablespoons brandy
1 cup whipping cream
salt

Melt the butter in a small saucepan. Add the shallot and sauté over medium heat until soft.

Add the mushrooms and sauté for 5 minutes, stirring frequently.

Add the parsley, peppercorns, and 2 to 3 drops of Tabasco sauce.

Warm the brandy and ignite it. Pour the brandy into the mushroom mixture and stir until the flames subside.

Add the cream. Boil the sauce, stirring constantly, until it thickens.

Add salt to taste.

BAKED STUFFED POTATOES

(8 servings)

4 large baking potatoes
vegetable oil
¼ cup butter
1 cup sour cream
salt and pepper
paprika

Preheat the oven to 400° F.

Rub the potatoes with a little oil.

Bake the potatoes at 400° F. for 1 hour or until done.

Cut the potatoes in half lengthwise and scoop out the potato. Reserve the potato shells.

Mash the potato with the butter, sour cream, and salt and pepper to taste. Stuff the potato shells with the mixture. Sprinkle lightly with paprika.

Place the potato halves in an ovenproof casserole.

Bake at 400° F. for 10 minutes or until lightly browned.

HOLIDAY TOMATOES

(8 servings)

8 tomatoes
¼ cup butter, divided
¼ cup celery, chopped
1 clove garlic, pressed
1 cup fine bread crumbs
1 teaspoon salt
¼ teaspoon pepper
2 tablespoons parsley, chopped
½ cup Parmesan cheese, grated, divided

Preheat the oven to 400° F.

Butter an ovenproof casserole.

Dip the tomatoes in boiling water for 30 seconds. Slip off the skins. Hollow out each center from the stem end, leaving a ½-inch shell. Sprinkle the shells lightly with salt. Turn the tomatoes upside down on a rack to drain for 15 minutes.

Melt 2 tablespoons of butter in a small skillet. Add the celery and garlic and sauté over medium heat until the vegetables are slightly soft.

Combine the bread crumbs, salt, pepper, parsley, and all but 2 tablespoons of the Parmesan. Add the sautéed celery and garlic. Mix well.

Place the tomatoes upright in the prepared casserole. Fill the centers with the stuffing. Sprinkle with the remaining cheese and dot with 2 tablespoons of butter.

Bake at 400° F. for 10 minutes.

FRENCH DRESSING

(see page 43)

VIENNESE CHOCOLATE TORTE

3 ounces unsweetened chocolate
½ cup butter
⅔ cup light brown sugar
⅔ cup dark brown sugar
3 eggs
1 teaspoon vanilla
1½ cups cake flour, sifted twice
2 teaspoons baking soda
⅛ teaspoon salt
½ cup buttermilk
½ cup boiling water
BUTTERCREAM *(page 139)*
CHOCOLATE GLAZE *(page 139)*
chocolate shavings (optional)

Preheat the oven to 350° F.

Grease well and lightly flour the bottom and sides of a 10-inch round cake pan. Line the bottom of the pan with a circle of waxed paper.

Melt the chocolate in the top of a double boiler over hot water.

Cream the butter and the light and dark brown sugars well.

Add the eggs, 1 at a time, beating well after each addition.

Add the melted chocolate and vanilla.

Sift the cake flour, baking soda, and salt together.

Add ½ of the dry ingredients to the chocolate mixture. Beat well.

Add the buttermilk, the remaining dry ingredients, and the boiling water, beating well after each addition.

Pour into the prepared pan.

Bake at 350° F. for 35 minutes or until done.

Cool in the pan for 10 minutes before turning out onto a rack.

After the cake is completely cool, slice it horizontally into three layers.

Spread the Coffee Buttercream over the bottom layer of the torte.

Place the second layer on top and spread it with ¼ of the Chocolate Buttercream.

Place the third layer on top.

Spread the top and sides of the torte with the remaining Chocolate Buttercream.

Place the torte in the freezer for 10 minutes.

In one motion pour the Chocolate Glaze over the torte, letting the glaze drip over the sides. Use a spatula to cover the sides with the glaze, touching the top only if necessary.

Cool.

Decorate the torte with the remaining 3 tablespoons of Chocolate Buttercream and add chocolate shavings if desired.

BUTTERCREAM

(2 cups)

4 egg yolks
⅔ cup sugar
3 tablespoons water
1 cup unsalted butter, softened
1 teaspoon vanilla
1 teaspoon instant coffee
2 teaspoons boiling water
3 ounces semisweet chocolate

Place the egg yolks in a medium sized bowl. Reserve.

Combine the sugar and water in a heavy saucepan. Swirl the mixture over medium heat until the sugar dissolves. Do not stir. Boil to the soft-ball stage (238° F.). Remove from the heat.

While beating the egg yolks, slowly pour the hot syrup over them. Beat until the mixture is cool.

Add the softened butter bit by bit, beating only until creamy.

Add the vanilla.

Place ¼ of the buttercream in a small bowl and ¾ in a medium bowl.

Dissolve the instant coffee in the boiling water. Beat it into the ¼ portion of the buttercream.

Melt the chocolate in the top of a double boiler over hot water. Add it to the ¾ portion of buttercream. Reserve 3 heaping tablespoons of the chocolate buttercream for decoration if desired.

CHOCOLATE GLAZE

(1 cup)

8 ounces semisweet chocolate
¼ cup butter

Melt the chocolate and butter together in the top of a double boiler over hot water. Cool slightly.

Index

Entries in *italics* refer to illustrations on facing page unless otherwise noted

Index

Index